Interdisciplinary Teaching and Teacher Education

Interdisciplinary Teaching and Teacher Education

Developing Teacher Competencies for Interdisciplinary Instruction

Edited by
Jiwon Kim
Sandra Zak

ROWMAN & LITTLEFIELD
Lanham • Boulder • New York • London

Published by Rowman & Littlefield
An imprint of The Rowman & Littlefield Publishing Group, Inc.
4501 Forbes Boulevard, Suite 200, Lanham, Maryland 20706
www.rowman.com

86-90 Paul Street, London EC2A 4NE, United Kingdom

Copyright © 2025 by Jiwon Kim and Sandra Zak

All rights reserved. No part of this book may be reproduced in any form or by any electronic or mechanical means, including information storage and retrieval systems, without written permission from the publisher, except by a reviewer who may quote passages in a review.

British Library Cataloguing in Publication Information Available

Library of Congress Cataloging-in-Publication Data

Names: Kim, Jiwon, 1975– editor. | Zak, Sandra, 1967– editor.
Title: Interdisciplinary teaching and teacher education : developing teacher competencies for interdisciplinary instruction / Edited by Jiwon Kim, Sandra Zak.
Description: Lanham, Maryland : Rowman & Littlefield, [2025] | Includes bibliographical references.
Summary: "Teaching and Teacher Education: Developing Teacher Competencies for Interdisciplinary Instruction introduces interdisciplinary education to teachers and teacher educators"— Provided by publisher.
Identifiers: LCCN 2024038054 (print) | LCCN 2024038055 (ebook) | ISBN 9781475871593 (cloth) | ISBN 9781475871609 (paperback) | ISBN 9781475871616 (epub)
Subjects: LCSH: Interdisciplinary approach in education. | Teachers—Training of. | Teachers—In-service training. | Motivation in education.
Classification: LCC LB2361 .I495 2025 (print) | LCC LB2361 (ebook) | DDC 707.1—dc23/eng/20240821
LC record available at https://lccn.loc.gov/2024038054
LC ebook record available at https://lccn.loc.gov/2024038055

∞™ The paper used in this publication meets the minimum requirements of American National Standard for Information Sciences—Permanence of Paper for Printed Library Materials, ANSI/NISO Z39.48-1992.

Contents

Foreword *John E. Henning*		vii
Acknowledgments		ix
1	Introduction to Interdisciplinary Education *Jiwon Kim*	1
2	Interdisciplinary Elementary Teacher Preparation *Jiwon Kim, Sandra Zak, and Vecihi Serbay Zambak*	11
3	Planning an Elementary Interdisciplinary Unit *Christine Grabowski*	25
4	Interdisciplinary Instruction Supports Thinking and Writing *Hank Bitten*	39
5	An Interdisciplinary Approach for Secondary Schools *Hank Bitten and Mark Pearcy*	51
6	Conclusion *Sandra Zak*	67
About the Editors and Authors		71

Foreword

John E. Henning

Interdisciplinary education lifts students beyond the confines of individual subject matter boundaries. Designing instructional units that simultaneously address multiple disciplines can provide a richer, more complex environment that optimizes interdisciplinary thinking. It's the kind of thinking needed to solve the type of real-world problems that rarely occur within a single discipline. It causes learners to engage in a more complex analysis of a topic that results in a deeper, more integrated understanding. And as the authors aptly note, the emphasis on inquiry and real-world problem-solving often makes learning more interesting, more relevant, and more engaging than traditional disciplinary instruction.

Despite its many benefits, interdisciplinary instruction is often overlooked. Perhaps that is to be expected, considering the complexity of integrating multiple subjects into a single unit of instruction. To do so requires a set of skills that transcend traditional disciplinary instruction. Teachers must be knowledgeable in multiple content areas and must know how each of those subjects informs the topic at hand. Further, they must know how to plan for incorporating multiple disciplinary perspectives into a single unit, how to create processes that engage students in interdisciplinary work, and how to assess the complexity of their students' work. Ideally, preparatory instruction should be provided to preservice teachers during their teacher education programs, and multiple examples of interdisciplinary units must be shared with practicing teachers as part of their professional development opportunities.

That is why this book is so useful. It approaches interdisciplinary education at the preservice, elementary, and secondary school levels of teaching. For teacher educators, there is a chapter on how to create a curriculum with the content knowledge and the practical experiences needed for interdisciplinary teaching. For teachers, an elementary teacher shows how she uses literature as a springboard for inspiring and then organizing her interdisciplinary units. In chapter 2 for elementary teachers, multiple examples are given for making connections across disciplines, especially English Language Arts, Social Studies, Science, and the Arts. Another chapter addresses the challenges of interdisciplinary instruction at the secondary level by showing how both courses and subject matter can be integrated.

This book will resonate with teachers, teacher educators, and educational leaders. Its ideas and strategies have been tested and proven successful in classrooms at both the P–12 and college levels. In large part, I attribute the authors' success to their extensive collaboration in interdisciplinary education across disciplinary boundaries, grade levels, and through school and university partnerships. The creativity spawned by their conversations is reflected throughout the chapters in this book. That collaboration has also helped them enjoy many of the same benefits from interdisciplinary learning as their students, while simultaneously positioning them to serve as excellent role models.

Finally, I am the former dean of School of Education, where much of this work took place. So, I was able to observe first-hand the knowledge and commitment of these educators and authors. They are highly dedicated to interdisciplinary education. Enjoy and appreciate their work.

John E. Henning
Professor Emeritus
Monmouth University

Acknowledgments

This book is the outcome of a group of educators sharing their ideas to reshape our future classrooms. We began with a goal to help our elementary education teacher candidates be well-prepared for teaching multiple subjects and undertaking interdisciplinary instruction in their future classrooms. While working with in-service teachers through workshops and stakeholder groups for climate change education, however, we realized the importance and possibility of this method in secondary schools and their teacher training programs as well. We want to thank and individually acknowledge all the incredible authors who joined us for this purpose in writing this book and shared their expertise in these different grade levels and pre- and in-serve teacher training.

Christine Grabowski in the Hazlet school district has been a long-time proponent of the interdisciplinary method of teaching, bringing it to her elementary classrooms many years ago. Her dedication to the method shows not only in her chapter but also in the time she gives to the course offered at Monmouth University on teaching the interdisciplinary method. Every year, she comes to the class to help introduce and show what is possible with this method.

Hank Bitten of the New Jersey Council for the Social Studies has also worked tirelessly to bring the interdisciplinary teaching method to both his classrooms at the elementary and high school levels, along with various districts in New Jersey. His support of the method and using social studies as a natural place to begin reminds all of us of the importance of the subjects within the social studies discipline and the learning experience of the students.

Mark Pearcy at Rider University has started the first steps of showing secondary-level preservice teachers that while they may teach a variety of different subjects, they all have common concerns and aspects of the job that need to be addressed before they graduate. It is an exciting development for education courses to bring a variety of different academic subjects together and get them to see that they have more in common than differences, allowing them to make connections that they never would have and opening the door to more cross-curricular work.

Vecihi Serbay Zambak at Monmouth University took the lead in studying how the interdisciplinary studies in elementary education students scored on the Elementary Level Math Praxis compared to the mathematics majors pursuing a degree focused on teaching at the K–6 level. His research concludes the strength of the program and how important the work of this major is.

Finally, we would like to acknowledge all those who have supported us, the major, and our work over the past years. First, the Monmouth University faculty, staff, and administration who have promoted the major, the co-teaching model of the capstone course, and championed our work. Although this book stems from our research on our co-teaching capstone course for the interdisciplinary elementary teacher education major, we would not have become advocates for interdisciplinary education if it were not for Bonnie Gold and the Monmouth University's committee that was formed to develop the Interdisciplinary Studies for Elementary Education (ISEE) major ten years ago in 2014. The major was the innovative approach as a result of collective efforts of multiple faculty members and the deans from the School of Education, School of Science, and School of Humanities and Social Sciences.

We also acknowledge the school districts, especially those who responded to our need to study for the new program, and Hazlet Public Schools and Ridgewood Public Schools, which shared their exemplary practice of interdisciplinary education. There are many individuals whose academic work has inspired us and our teacher-candidate students through guest lectures in the capstone course: Sohyun An, Rico Gutstein, Grace Lasker, Zaneta Rago-Craft, Catherine Duckett, Andrea VanDeusen, Kimberly Callas, and Amanda Beecher.

We are also grateful for the support received as we collected data for this study from our graduate assistants, Gabrielle Ojeda, Hadgu Hadgu, Brittney Henry, Rachel Peyser, and Olivia Ababio, and for the manuscript support from Danielle Kim Lee. Most of all, we are profoundly appreciative of our teacher-candidate students who explored with us foundational questions—what teachers need to teach and how they should teach—and shared their brilliantly designed interdisciplinary work with us.

Lastly, both of us would like to thank our families, whose support and love were instrumental in giving us the time and strength to finish.

Chapter 1

Introduction to Interdisciplinary Education

Jiwon Kim

UNDERSTANDING INTERDISCIPLINARY EDUCATION

Teachers teach not just subjects, but people. Therefore, teachers need to bridge subject content with interests, cultures, and issues that students live with within their homes, community, and world.

Because real-world problems are not divided as a math block or language arts block may be, interdisciplinary instruction could help students better understand topics in a more realistic, familiar, and complete context and coherently use various subject knowledge and skills wherever they need to solve problems. Many problems are especially relevant to global challenges, and those issues need interdisciplinary solutions that require working together. Using a variety of methods and reforming the way we teach and assess students also play a crucial role.

While traditional instruction tends to isolate academic disciplines or subject areas from one another, interdisciplinary instruction always begins with a central topic, theme, or problem that instructors select through scanning cross-curricular standards or guide students in pursuing their inquiry, depending on the student's level and the learning goals.

The particularity of interdisciplinary instruction is the integration of notions and guiding principles from multiple disciplines to systematically form a more complete framework of analysis that offers a richer understanding of the issue under examination. In K–12 classroom's interdisciplinary instruction, the theme or topic is more teacher-directed and curriculum-based, but the interdisciplinary method is the same for meaningful learning because it amplifies what students learn by allowing them to tackle problems that don't fit neatly into one subject area. It also changes how students learn by asking them to blend and reflect on multiple perspectives instead of accepting a teacher's perspective unquestioningly (Ahire, 2022).

In this process, interdisciplinary instruction is also enabling students to engage with this learning process with more eagerness and achieve a deeper understanding, while encouraging them to be receptive to new concepts and ideas. It helps students become more internally motivated to study and learn because, as Dewey (1916) said, students want to hear and understand only when the subject does "touch them" or "enter into their concerns" by teachers' "arousing interests or bringing about a sense of connection" (p. 129).

There is multiple evidence of the observable benefits of interdisciplinary education provided by recent research (An et al., 2013; Brand & Triplett, 2012; Santau & Ritter, 2013). By connecting different areas of study, interdisciplinary education aims to facilitate greater conceptual understanding in students than if they had learned content from each subject in isolation (Brand & Triplett, 2012; Campbell & Henning, 2010; Gerke, 2017) and develop a more powerful understanding of complex problems, greater enthusiasm, breadth and depth of information, problem-solving skills, critical thinking skills, and meaningful application of knowledge and skills. It is reported that students learning in interdisciplinary settings showed higher achievement, improved memory, and performed better on state tests, as well as had greater social outcomes than students learning the same content without an interdisciplinary approach (Cunnington et al., 2014). In addition to the better understanding of content, students also develop a sense of pride and empowerment (Muthersbaugh et al., 2014). As for teachers, it allows for a more efficient use of class time, especially with limited instructional hours for social studies and science, and differentiation for diverse learners.

DEFINITIONS

The term "interdisciplinary education" does not have a single definition that is accepted by researchers and practitioners. As Applebee et al. (2007, p. 1,005) noted, "there is little consensus on terms and definitions to describe how different disciplines relate to one another and very little cross-referencing among authors who address issues in interdisciplinary studies." This lack of consensus makes defining and implementing interdisciplinary education challenging. But, as the Lucas Education Research Institution reported (Warkentien et al., 2022), although the several definitions incorporate slightly different language, commonalities exist across each of these definitions (Boix Mansilla, 2005; Drake & Burns, 2004; Moser et al., 2020; National Academy of Sciences, 2004; Newell, 2013) that point to an emerging consensus definition:

> First, interdisciplinary education requires disciplines as these are the foundation upon which insights and learning are made (Szostak, 2015). Second, it must draw on more than one discipline as part of its substantive focus (i.e., the focus must require more than a single perspective). Third, interdisciplinary education must involve an explicit integration of the disciplines so that the learner is solving a problem, addressing an issue, answering a question, explaining a phenomenon, or creating a new product. (Warkentien et al., 2022, I–6)

Interdisciplinary, multidisciplinary, and integrated education are the most used and similar ways in terms of their involving more than one discipline or subject area. In the sense of all involving attention to more than a single academic discipline or subject area, they are all *interdisciplinary*. However, they differ in specific ways of planning and teaching. First, integrated instruction incorporates one subject within others. Although multidisciplinary instruction makes use of two or more disciplines or subject areas, one teacher or a team of teachers work in parallel, sequentially, or jointly, from their specific disciplines based on addressing a common topic or problem. Interdisciplinary instruction is planned by one teacher, involving students "in exploration of comprehensive interdisciplinary or multidisciplinary studies of topics, themes, or problems," "commonly organized as activity-centered units," so it is usually most appropriate for elementary and middle schools (Wood, 2015, p. 5).

As exemplary approaches to interdisciplinary education, inquiry-based learning is often cited and used at all grade levels because it aims to increase student motivation and engagement as well as connect student learning to its real-life application. Inquiry-based learning is a family of three similar approaches, which are project-based learning, problem-based learning, and design-based learning (Barron & Darling-Hammond, 2008). All three models approach issues in an interdisciplinary and thematic fashion because their focus on authentic and meaningful problems requires interdisciplinary reflection. The terms inquiry-based learning and inquiry-based education have appeared with increasing frequency in educational policy and curriculum documents over the past decade, indicating a major educational trend (Artigue & Blomhøj, 2013). The origin of inquiry is a pedagogical concept in the work of Dewey (1916). Dewey's concept of reflective thinking, which involves a state of uncertainty and perplexity and an act of searching and inquiring (Dewey, 1933) has been the central foundation undergirding inquiry-based learning. And,

The approach now stands upon the shoulders of Piaget, Vygotsky, and Bruner, and continues to dominate educational landscapes and inquiry-based approaches to teaching and learning have, in contemporary forms, withstood the test of time, influencing problem-based and place-based methodology and reflecting influences of social and cognitive constructivism, humanistic psychology, and eco-feminism. (Herman & Pinard, 2015)

Interdisciplinary education, which is often conducted through inquiry-based learning, is widely recommended in curriculum integration, practice, and school reform in many countries around the world (Thorburn, 2017) and through the U.S. national and state standards, such as the National Science Education Standards (NSES) and the National Council for the Social Studies (NCSS). In reality, however, inquiry-based learning has not been fully understood and, hence, not implemented (Evancho, 2022; Won, 2009).

INTERDISCIPLINARY EDUCATION IN SCHOOLS

Reports on interdisciplinary programs in schools have been and continue to be limited, and there is a lack of adequate research or guidance on methods (Lagemann & Shulman, 1999; Warkentien et al., 2022; Wood, 2015). Several factors that may facilitate or inhibit the implementation of interdisciplinary education include: principal support that gives teachers time and resources to develop and deliver interdisciplinary units, teacher motivation and commitment to interdisciplinary instruction, and a collaborative teaching environment. Whereas factors inhibiting interdisciplinary educational approaches are standards and accountability policies that narrow the curriculum and put pressure on raising achievement in discrete disciplines and rigid school structures that prevent sufficient planning time or teacher collaboration opportunities. In addition, training pre- and in-service teachers to become familiar with this approach is rare.

Due to these factors, in many cases interdisciplinary education approaches can be found only within some schools and with some teachers, but the overall reach is extremely limited and implemented very unevenly. A few other case studies and interviews (Gerke, 2017; Tonnetti & Lentillon-Kaestner, 2023) support these findings and particularly note that the teacher is the central factor. First, the teacher's knowledge plays a role in effective interdisciplinary education implementation (Gardner & Tillotson, 2019; Gerke, 2017; Pearson, 2017). Integrating the curriculum is challenging; many teachers were not educated as students in interdisciplinary ways, have little training in designing interdisciplinary units, and may not feel prepared to extend beyond their disciplinary expertise (Caskey, 2002; Weinberg &

Sample McMeeking, 2017; Wang et al., 2020; Wu et al., 2021). A systematic review (Tonnetti & Lentillon, 2023) of teaching interdisciplinarity in secondary school more clearly shows these obstacles. Few interdisciplinary practices are used in secondary schools, and even fewer achieve a real integration of disciplines. In addition to teacher knowledge, teacher motivation and confidence are important considerations in whether a school or teaching team is ready for interdisciplinary instruction (Applebee et al., 2007). Without a deep commitment to the work, implementation is not likely to succeed.

Therefore, teacher preparation and professional development are critical. The teacher certification system and teacher training program prioritize single-subject-area expertise and place little focus on the integration of subjects during preservice preparation (Gardner & Tillotson, 2019). Scholars have called for many more opportunities for teacher preparation and professional development and a more thorough examination of how preservice teacher preparation and in-service teacher professional development affect the implementation and impacts of interdisciplinary education (Harrison et al., 2020). As noted by Havice et al. (2018), an interdisciplinary (or integrated) approach cannot occur "overnight," particularly not without thoughtful training for current and future teachers. Superficial connections result in part from teachers' discomfort or unfamiliarity with subject matter. A potential solution to this problem, especially in secondary schools, may be collaboration between teachers with different areas of expertise, which they can combine to design integrated lessons (Carrier et al., 2011). Teachers who practice interdisciplinary instruction highlight collaboration with colleagues as a key part of developing competence in planning and implementing an interdisciplinary curriculum (Gerke, 2017). Recommendations arising from all these studies are that teacher education should explicitly address interdisciplinary education.

Though students need this perspective and these skills early on, it is not just applicable to K–12 students but also to teacher-candidate students who will teach with this new instructional approach as well. Teachers may naturally be inclined toward their own areas of knowledge or expertise (Ahire, 2022). Many teachers who practice interdisciplinary education identified (Warkentien et al., 2022) numerous roadblocks to the wide adoption of interdisciplinary approaches, primarily focusing on accountability and testing structures that govern so many instructional decisions in districts and schools (Warkentien et al., 2022). These affect the capacity of educators (time and training) to pivot to a new instructional approach, which was a secondary concern. Teachers, especially in secondary education, are trained in their disciplines and are typically very comfortable teaching the value of their discipline to students. Asking teachers to go beyond their comfort zone into substantive areas that they are either unfamiliar with or would require close collaboration with other teachers is challenging.

Moreover, teachers have incredible responsibilities and requirements without adding the challenge of learning, designing, and implementing a new instructional approach that might require new ways of teaching, collaborating, and significant professional development.

OVERVIEW OF THIS BOOK

The purpose of this book is to provide pre-service and in-service teachers and teacher educators with showcases of the implementing process. There are studies and books that focus on the planning process related to interdisciplinary education (Drake & Burns, 2004; Wood, 2015), but little that show the implementing process or explore how teachers or teacher educators reflect on and revise their curriculum. Teachers and teacher educators need to see how others have implemented and gained understanding, confidence, and motivation.

This book offers multiple examples of real teachers' and teacher educators' interdisciplinary education practices, to help many other teachers and teacher educators learn this approach and gain the knowledge, skills, and confidence to use them for implementation in their own classrooms at any level. This book explains how interdisciplinary learning is blended into primary and secondary education, and how higher educational frameworks must be shaped by the intended objective of interdisciplinary education.

Chapter 2 reviews a complete example that explains the process involved in a preservice teacher education program, which is named Interdisciplinary Studies for Elementary Educators (ISEE) major. The chapter discusses how this major was created and has taught knowledge and skills for interdisciplinary education for several years, and how the preservice teacher-candidate students have gained self-efficacy for interdisciplinary teaching.

Chapter 3 provides us with another way to look at designing and implementing interdisciplinary units from a master teacher's experience in her elementary school classroom. This chapter details the steps required in planning the teacher's interdisciplinary unit plans that she created by using the backward design model, cross-curricular standards, and graphic organizers and then teaching and assessing students. This review also shows how this teacher's interdisciplinary instruction has assisted her students with powerful learning experiences over many years.

In chapter 4, a former teacher and curriculum developer discusses several different models of interdisciplinary education, with a more systematic explanation of how multiple subjects standards can be covered in interdisciplinary instruction. For each model, exemplary units about current and global issues are illustrated.

Chapter 5 is specially designed to discuss the possibility of an interdisciplinary approach at the secondary level and preparation for middle and high school teachers. This chapter proposes and explains one way of doing it, with integration around social studies, but discusses in what other ways teachers can overcome their disciplinary identity, get prepared, collaborate with other teachers, and create a fully interdisciplinary course.

Each chapter includes details of real examples and thorough explanations of the process and reflection on implementing them. This information can serve students and educators as references and guidance.

REFERENCES

Ahire, B. (2022). The future of education is interdisciplinary. Retrieved March 15, 2024, https://www.k12digest.com/the-future-of-education-is-interdisciplinary/

An, S., Capraro, M. M. & Tillman, D. A. (2013). Elementary teachers integrate music activities into regular mathematics lessons: Effects on students' mathematical abilities. *Journal for Learning through the Arts, 9*(1), 1–19.

Applebee, A. N., Adler, M. & Flihan, S. (2007). Interdisciplinary curricula in middle and high school classrooms. *American Educational Research Journal, 44*(4), 1002–1039.

Artigue, M. & Blomhøj, M. (2013). Conceptualizing inquiry-based education in mathematics. *Zdm, 45*(6), 797–810.

Barron, B. & Darling-Hammond, L. (2008). How can we teach for meaningful learning? In L. Darling-Hammond (Ed.), *Powerful pedagogy: What we know about teaching for understanding.* San Francisco, CA: John Wiley & Sons. 11–70.

Boix Mansilla, V. (2005). Assessing student work at disciplinary crossroads. *Change Magazine, 37*(1), 14–21.

Brand, B. R. & Triplett, C. F. (2012). Interdisciplinary curriculum: An abandoned concept? *Teachers and Teaching, 18*(3), 381–393.

Campbell, C. & Henning, M. B. (2010). Planning, teaching, and assessing elementary education interdisciplinary curriculum. *International Journal of Teaching and Learning in Higher Education, 22*(2), 179–186.

Carrier, S., Gray, P., Wiebe, E. N. & Teachout, D. (2011). BioMusic in the classroom: Interdisciplinary elementary science and music curriculum development. *School Science and Mathematics, 111*(8), 425–434.

Caskey, M. (2002). A lingering question for middle school: What is the fate of integrated curriculum? Issues in education. *Childhood Education, 78*(2), 97–99.

Cunnington, M., Kantrowitz, A., Harnett, S. & Hill-Ries, A. (2014). Cultivating common ground: Integrating standards-based visual arts, math, and literacy in high-poverty urban classrooms. *Journal for Learning through the Arts, 10*(1), 1–24.

Dewey, J. (1916). *Democracy and education.* New York, NY: Free Press.

Dewey, J. (1933). *How we think*. Boston, New York: Houghton Mifflin Co.
Drake, S. M. & Burns, R. C. (2004). *Meeting standards through integrated curriculum*. Alexandria, VA: ASCD.
Evancho, T. (2022). *The impact of the C3 framework on state social studies standards*. [Unpublished doctoral dissertation]. Monmouth University.
Gardner, M. & Tillotson, J. W. (2019). Interpreting integrated STEM: Sustaining pedagogical innovation within a public middle school context. *International Journal of Science and Mathematics Education, 17*(7), 1283–1300.
Gerke, A. G. (2017). *Interdisciplinary education in the elementary curriculum: Exploring teacher perceptions and practices*. [Unpublished master's thesis]. Ontario Institute for Studies in Education of the University of Toronto.
Harrison, L. M., Hurd, E. & Brinegar, K. (Eds.). (2020). *Integrative and interdisciplinary curriculum in the middle school: Integrated approaches in teacher preparation and practice*. Oxfordshire: Routledge Research in Education.
Havice, W., Havice, P., Waugaman, C. & Walker, K. (2018). Evaluating the effectiveness of integrative STEM education: Teacher and administrator professional development. *Journal of Technology Education, 29*(2), 73–90.
Herman, W. E. & Pinard, M. R. (2015). Critically examining inquiry-based learning: John Dewey in theory, history, and practice. In *Inquiry-based learning for multidisciplinary programs: A conceptual and practical resource for educators*. Leeds: Emerald Group Publishing Limited. *Innovations in Higher Education Teaching and Learning, 3,* 43–62.
Lagemann, E. C. & Shulman, L. S. (1999). *Issues in educational research: Problems and possibilities*. San Francisco: Jossey-Bass.
Moser, K. M., Ivy, J. & Hopper, P. F. (2020). Rethinking content teaching at the middle level: An interdisciplinary approach. In L. M. Harrison, E. Hurd, & K. Brinegar (Eds.), *Integrative and interdisciplinary curriculum in the middle school: Integrated approaches in teacher preparation and practice*. Oxfordshire: Routledge Research in Education. 113–128.
Muthersbaugh, D., Kern, A. L. & Charvoz, R. (2014). Impact through images: Exploring student understanding of environmental science through integrated place-based lessons in the elementary classroom. *Journal of Research in Childhood Education, 28*, 313–326.
National Academy of Sciences, National Academy of Engineering, and Institute of Medicine. (2004). *Facilitating interdisciplinary research*. Washington, DC: The National Academies Press.
Newell, W. H. (2013). The state of the field: Interdisciplinary theory. *Issues in Interdisciplinary Studies, 31*, 22–43.
Pearson, G. (2017). National academies piece on integrated STEM. *Journal of Educational Research, 110*(3), 224–226.
Santau, A. O. & Ritter, J. K. (2013). What to teach and how to teach it: Elementary teachers' views on teaching inquiry-based, interdisciplinary science and social studies in urban settings. *The New Educator, 9*(4), 255–286.
Szostak, R. (2015). Extensional definition of interdisciplinarity. *Issues in Interdisciplinary Studies, 33*, 94–116.

Thorburn, M. (2017). Dewey, democracy, and interdisciplinary learning: A Scottish perspective. *Oxford Review of Education, 43*(2), 242–254.

Tonnetti, B. & Lentillon-Kaestner, V. (2023). Teaching interdisciplinarity in secondary school: A systematic review, *Cogent Education, 10*(1), 2216038. https://doi.org/10.1080/2331186X.2023.2216038

Wang, H. H., Charoenmuang, M., Knoblock, N. A. & Tormoehlen, R. L. (2020). Defining interdisciplinary collaboration based on high school teachers' beliefs and practices of STEM integration using a complex designed system. *International Journal of STEM Education, 7*(3).

Warkentien, S., Goeking, J., Dilig, R., Knapp, L. & Stanley, R. (2022). *Interdisciplinary education: Literature review and landscape analysis*. Washington, DC: Lucas Education Research International.

Weinberg, A. E. & Sample McMeeking, L. B. (2017). Toward meaningful interdisciplinary education: High school teachers' views of mathematics and science integration. *School Science and Mathematics, 117*(5), 204–213.

Won, M. (2009). *Issues in inquiry-based science education seen through Dewey's theory of inquiry*. [Unpublished doctoral dissertation]. University of Illinois at Urbana-Champaign.

Wood, K. (2015). *Interdisciplinary instruction: Unit and lesson planning strategies K–8* (5th ed). Long Grove, IL: Waveland Press, Inc.

Wu, Y., Cheng, J. & Koszalka, T. A. (2021). Transdisciplinary approach in middle school: A case study of co-teaching practices in STEAM teams. *International Journal of Education in Mathematics, Science and Technology, 9*(1), 138–162.

Chapter 2

Interdisciplinary Elementary Teacher Preparation

Jiwon Kim, Sandra Zak, and Vecihi Serbay Zambak

BACKGROUND

Elementary school generalist teachers must be prepared to teach all four major core subjects: language arts, mathematics, social studies, and science. Thus, teacher candidates need significant preparation beyond high school in all four areas. They must have a depth of knowledge in these fields that will permit them to make appropriate pedagogical decisions. They need to understand how the fields fit together, what concepts must be taught prior to others, and what skills their students need to develop to learn the concepts. They must be able to evaluate textbooks in each field and prepare assessments of their students' learning.

Many elementary teacher preparation programs are content-area majors, but some universities and states require interdisciplinary or multidisciplinary majors for future generalist elementary teachers.[1] Rising standards set by teacher preparation accreditation bodies are likely to compel a growing number of states to require interdisciplinary programs at the college level for students intending to be generalist teachers.

This chapter showcases an interdisciplinary major of Monmouth University in New Jersey. While the Interdisciplinary Studies for Elementary Educators (ISEE) program is housed in the Department of Curriculum and Instruction in the School of Education, the program itself is a joint project of the Schools of Education, Humanities and Social Sciences, and Science, and is supervised and directed by committee members from all three schools. Students pursuing the program gain a deeper knowledge of the material that they will later teach by studying each area in five to nine courses at the college level. The state of New Jersey requires all preservice teachers to have a major in an academic discipline in addition to taking appropriate education courses and fulfilling general education requirements. When the academic discipline is a single subject, the total number of credits required to meet all these expectations leaves students with no available credits to take more than the minimum in any other field. The ISEE program, by contrast, gives graduates some of the depth that students gain in individual majors through sequences of five to nine courses in each area that require the students' level of understanding to grow, while still giving students the breadth they need to be effective elementary teachers.

PRINCIPLES OF THE ISEE PROGRAM

The ISEE major provides significant coursework at the university level to better prepare future elementary teachers in each of the four subject areas they will teach. The curriculum includes five courses in mathematics, five courses in science, six courses in reading and language arts, and nine courses in social studies. Fifteen or more credit hours in each of these areas help prepare future teachers to be highly qualified in all areas, including helping students prepare to pass all four subject-area PRAXIS II exams required by New Jersey. Elementary teachers with high levels of proficiency in all subject areas are better equipped to help their students meet learning outcomes associated with the Common Core State Standards and the New Jersey Student Learning Standards.

The ISEE curriculum was constructed with reference to relevant standards and recommendations made by professional organizations. Some of these include the Common Core State Standards for Mathematics (CCSS-M), the National Council of Teachers of Mathematics (NCTM), Next Generation Science Standards (NGSS), and the PRAXIS II social studies and reading/language arts content. Additionally, the major is a cooperative endeavor involving Arts and Sciences units and the School of Education. ISEE content-area courses are delivered by Arts and Sciences departments and faculty. ISEE content-area courses are augmented by pedagogy-focused courses in mathematics, science, language arts, and social studies. Methods courses outside the ISEE major are delivered by School of Education faculty. The ISEE capstone course is delivered by both Arts and Sciences and School of Education faculty. Administration of the ISEE major is housed in the Department of Curriculum and Instruction of the School of Education.

This cooperative effort between Arts and Sciences and the School of Education helps meet expectations set by the Council for the Accreditation of Educator Preparation (CAEP), the national body responsible for the accreditation of teacher education programs. CAEP and its predecessors, the National Council for Accreditation of Teacher Education (NCATE) and the

Teacher Education Accreditation Council (TEAC), require accredited teacher education institutions to provide demonstrably strong content-area curricula as well as other training experiences normally provided by schools of education (e.g., clinical placements and pedagogy-focused coursework).

EFFECTIVENESS OF INTERDISCIPLINARY ELEMENTARY TEACHER PREPARATION

How should future elementary teachers be prepared for the profession? What knowledge should elementary teacher candidates demonstrate or develop prior to their first year of teaching? Every elementary teacher education program in the United States differently answers these questions with their required coursework and provided teaching and learning experiences for teacher candidates. Professional teaching and subject-specific standards, at the same time, provide the guiding force in establishing a baseline for breadth and depth of elementary teacher education programs. For instance, the National Board for Professional Teaching Standards [NBPTS] (2012a) recommends ten standards for the teachers of students ages 3–10, one of which specifically underlines the importance of having subject matter knowledge in language and literacy, mathematics, science, and social studies to teach young children. NBPTS (2012b) also highlights similar content knowledge and curriculum standards for the teachers of students ages 7–12. Developing subject matter knowledge for teacher candidates during their preservice teacher education similarly supports their pedagogical content knowledge (Morris & Hiebert 2017).

Nonetheless, not all teacher education programs provide well-rounded opportunities for elementary teacher candidates to develop necessary content knowledge. According to the teacher quality review by Greenberg et al. (2013), 83 out of 692 (i.e., 12 percent of) elementary teacher education programs in the United States earned a strong design designation for the Early Reading Content Preparation standard. Brenner and McQuirk (2019) further pointed out that very few teacher education programs require elementary teacher candidates to take English Language Arts courses specifically focusing on children's literature or writing. Regarding required mathematics courses, only 130 out of 820 (i.e., 25 percent of) elementary education programs in the United States addressed essential mathematics topics in adequate breadth and depth with their coursework (Greenberg et al. 2013). Based on these findings, the authors concluded that mathematics courses offered to elementary teacher candidates are not strongly designed to cover full K–8 mathematics content. Other studies (e.g., Fonseca et al. 2018; Rech et al. 1993) similarly showed evidence of elementary teacher candidates' limited preparation and lack of mathematical competency to teach elementary mathematics.

Elementary teachers' preparation to teach science or social studies in K–6 grades is also limited. In her survey study, Trygstad (2013) found that fewer than half of the teacher education programs had at least one course in physics or chemistry, whereas the majority of the science coursework required life and earth sciences. The image for elementary teacher preparation to teach social studies is not very different (Mimbs 2002; Passe 2006; Womac 2014). Mimbs (2002) found that 32 percent of the programs that participated in her study did not require a geography course within their elementary teacher education programs. The status of geography courses within the elementary teacher education curriculum was even worse in 2014; Womac (2014) also found that 87 percent of the undergraduate elementary teacher education programs did not require their teacher candidates to take a geography course.

In light of these reports and studies, we believe ISEE undergraduate program provides sound content preparation for elementary teacher candidates with its balanced curriculum and coursework focusing on the breadth, depth, and interdisciplinarity of the contents of English Language Arts, mathematics, science, and social studies. To analyze the ISEE students' gains, subject-specific content knowledge, and teaching performance in comparison to the other elementary education programs offered by Monmouth University, we conducted statistical analyses on final Praxis 2 Test (and Subtest) scores and edTPA scores of elementary students (N = 266) who completed the program between the fall 2017 and spring 2022 semesters. Based on the program completed, we also compared the number of times students had to take Praxis and edTPA tests to meet the state's passing score requirements. Table 2.1 presents the number of elementary education students who completed different programs at Monmouth University within our data.

The results from the Analysis of Variance Test indicated that ISEE students had significantly higher Praxis 2 Math Subtest (5003) ($F(259, 6) = 2.914$; $p = 0.009$) and edTPA scores ($F(254, 6) = 2.141$; $p = 0.049$) in comparison to the other six programs categorized as in table 2.1. The LSD post hoc analyses revealed that the ISEE program was more effective in preparing elementary education students for the Praxis 2 Math Subtest compared to the students majored in undergraduate English Language Arts ($p = 0.005$), history ($p = 0.17$), and graduate MAT programs ($p = 0.048$). We also ran Independent Samples T-tests between each pair of programs, which also showed that ISEE students had significantly higher Praxis 2 Science Subtest (5005) scores in comparison to students majored in anthropology ($t(66) = 2.365$; $p = 0.010$) and English Language Arts programs ($t(72) = 2.014$; $p = 0.024$), together with elementary education. The ISEE students also had to take the Praxis 2 Social Studies Subtest (5004) significantly less than students majored in

Table 2.1. The Distribution of Elementary Education Programs within the Data.

Elementary Education Program	Number of Students (n)
Bachelor of Arts (BA) in Anthropology and Elementary Education	25
BA in English Language Arts and Elementary Education	80
BA in History and Elementary Education	24
BA in ISEE	43
Bachelor of Science in Mathematics and Elementary Education	11
MAT in Teaching, Elementary Education	73
Other (e.g., BA in Arts, early childhood education, music, or Spanish and elementary education)	10
TOTAL	266

anthropology ($t(32) = -1.796$; $p = 0.041$) and English Language Arts programs ($t(112) = -2.043$; $p = 0.022$), together with elementary education.

Based on these preliminary findings, we believe the ISEE program provides better opportunities for elementary teacher candidates to develop robust teaching skills and content knowledge, especially in mathematics and science subjects. It is likely that the ISEE program's balanced curriculum, with a focus on four subjects and subject-specific pedagogies necessary for elementary teacher preparation, contributed to these results.

CAPSTONE COURSE: INTERDISCIPLINARY METHODS COURSE

The following portion of this chapter will describe how an interdisciplinary methods course has been implemented. The teacher candidates will have completed most of their content-area courses and many of their content-based methods courses, which provides a basis for them to learn interdisciplinary methods of teaching. While this capstone course is for a specialized elementary education major, the key ideas are adaptable to each individual method course.

The capstone course, by design, is to be taught jointly, with one faculty member from a content-area discipline and the other from the education area. Each semester the course is taught, a broad theme for the course is chosen. Example of themes would be social justice, environment, bullying, climate change, poverty, and urbanization.

The course is designed into smaller sections: The first section is an introduction to the method of interdisciplinary teaching. The class has a chance to read about the method. The second section of the course is about six weeks in length. During this time, a series of speakers are invited to speak with the class. One of the speakers is a current elementary school teacher who has successfully designed and implemented numerous interdisciplinary lessons in her classroom. The others are university faculty from each of the major academic fields, who discuss a variety of topics and ideas that are relevant to the semester's theme and have the potential to become interdisciplinary lessons. These lessons provide teacher candidates with the opportunity to see how one theme may be understood and taught from multiple different perspectives, which leads to showing how the theme may be taught in an interdisciplinary way. The third section is about five weeks of the course that are spent reading more about how to design interdisciplinary lessons and having each student prepare an interdisciplinary unit plan. Finally, the fourth and last section is two weeks and reserved for the students to give short presentations, including a short teaching demonstration of one part of their unit plan. Throughout the entire course, there are multiple assignments, reflections, and assessments, with feedback given by the instructors to develop the teacher candidates' understanding of the topic and the skills required for interdisciplinary instruction.

Phase 1: Introduction

The course begins right away with a variety of readings to do prior to the first class. Part of the readings are an overview of the interdisciplinary method, including a background, its connection to active learning, and touching on some of the basics of creating a lesson plan using this method. The rest of the readings come from our first guest speaker, who provides the students with actual lessons given in the classroom at a local elementary school. During the first class, we first take time to discuss the readings on the interdisciplinary method with the students. The second part is given to the guest, who discusses the interdisciplinary units taught over the past few years, how they designed the lessons, and also how they worked with both the administration and parents to have support in creating and delivering the lessons. At the end, the students have the chance to ask questions of the in-service elementary school teacher.

Phase 2: Topics

After the introduction, the next step is to give the students some ideas to create their interdisciplinary unit plan. This phase is crucial, as students up to this point have created lesson plans in other courses specific to one subject. With students in this course expected to produce unit plans using standards from most of the disciplines taught by elementary school teachers, it is crucial they see broad topic ideas. Over the next five weeks, guest lecturers, who are professors in mathematics, language arts, social studies, science, gender studies, and music/arts, bring topic ideas from each of their specific disciplines. The topics brought center on their own discipline, but they are general enough to connect to other areas as the students learn in the next section. To give a few examples, in the semesters where the theme was social justice, the math faculty member discussed food deserts in the Chicago area. The social studies faculty member discussed the history of diseases as they relate to racism to immigrants to America, specifically from Asian countries. Finally, the gender studies faculty member showed young children still view the occupations of engineering, fighter pilot, and others as male positions. These are just a few of the topics covered. Many more were brought to the students. The guest lecturers are given complete authority over how they wish to use their classroom time and any pre-class work. We do encourage them to assign readings for before the class and to assign discussion board questions for the students to get the students fully prepared for the lecture. The students are also asked to come prepared with at least three questions to pose after the speaker's presentation.

The preparation work is key for the students if the goal is for them to come out of the lectures with as much information as possible. They are able to connect with a topic, which you can start to see during the question period for the speakers. Often, students will ask the speakers how other disciplines might connect to an idea or activities that might be developed. These questions show that the first week is also working in the students' minds as they begin to think of the direction they would like to choose.

Phase 3: Unit Preparation

After the last guest speaks, the first real step of the course toward the student's unit preparation is assigned. A topic and a grade level from K–6 must be chosen and posted on our learning management system. There is no requirement on how specific it must be at this point, other than the grade level. To help the students, a broad topic is allowed, as most do not have deep content knowledge they need a topic that they have chosen. There is also inexperience of starting with a topic and producing a lesson plan, in a process known as "backward design."

During the initial week, students read and discuss an introductory reading on interdisciplinary methods. The reading introduces many new terms and ideas related to creating an interdisciplinary lesson. It is in this section that many of these new terms are not just discussed and studied more, but are put into practice to create their unit plans. One of the first is the idea of backward design. Other such terms will come into play in this section.

As mentioned above, in utilizing backward design in the creation of a lesson, first a broad topic or theme is chosen. The topics that teacher candidates chose for their teaching units were as follows:

- Resources: hunger, food, access, income, health
- Gender: gender in job, gender in STEM, inequality, rights
- Environment: climate change, climate justice, natural disasters, water sanitation and sustainability, pollution (ocean, water, air, land)
- Diversity: civil rights, racism, racial injustice, discrimination, identity, bullying, inclusion

From this point, essential questions to be answered in the lesson are used to help align the learning standards, goals, and assessments in the lessons and unit plan development. The alignment is very important, as an interdisciplinary lesson uses all the academic disciplines. With a topic chosen and submitted through the learning management system, the teacher candidates then spend the next few weeks learning more about their topic through a literature review, workshops for both the literature review and the standards, presentations on these, and finally reading more in depth on creating an interdisciplinary unit plan.

In the first class after choosing the topic, each student gives a short presentation on their topic, the grade level it is for, and the reason they chose it. After each presentation, there is a chance for feedback and questions. Many times, students are able to point out weaknesses and/or strengths in the topic choice. With the topic, a literature review on each topic is assigned. To help them get started on this, the rest of the course time is spent mentoring students to find background information on their topic. The students have minimum standards of references they will need, with an expectation of finding many more. With the most pressing questions and concerns addressed in the workshop, students continue the work outside of class, turning it in the following week.

With the literature reviews moving forward, articles on interdisciplinary teaching are read over the next few weeks. In these readings, many examples of unit plans are looked at, and some key features of creating the unit plan are studied in much more depth. Students see the need for essential questions in organizing which academic subjects are needed and where.

With these ideas, the students are ready for a workshop on the standards. In the workshop, students are grouped into grades, or grade bands, and given the task of looking at standards from a specific discipline. They spend time scanning the standards both vertically and horizontally, seeing how they are organized and how they are connected. After doing the work, short presentations are given by each group so that everyone can gain a better understanding of the different disciplines' standards, how they are organized, and eventually what concepts and skills can be meaningfully taught together cross-curricular.

At this point, the students have a much deeper understanding of the topic they chose, having done the literature review, and this allows them to focus on their topic. With the idea of essential questions and a better idea of different discipline standards, the concept of a web design is introduced through readings and by looking at a variety of examples. In class, we start by discussing the idea, focusing on what the students learned and then the reason why these might be useful. The rest of the class is dedicated to working on their web designs. The students are grouped so that they can work together and discuss how to begin the web design, connecting ideas. So, together they are creating each other's web designs and, more importantly, helping each other learn how to do it. There isn't sufficient in-class time for them to finish, so they continue to work on it after class.

Below you will find the web designs of two different students. The first student chose their topic as "Diversity" (see figure 2.1), and the second chose "Pollution" (see figure 2.2). Both are very broad topics covering many different possible lessons and standards. However, as with all the students, the broad topics narrow with research, grade level specification, and knowing the standards. Seeing their web designs shows how each of the students will connect the disciplines to the topic and each other and finally to write a unit plan.

Having finished their web designs outside of class, the students present them at the start of the next class. As in the past presentation, students see

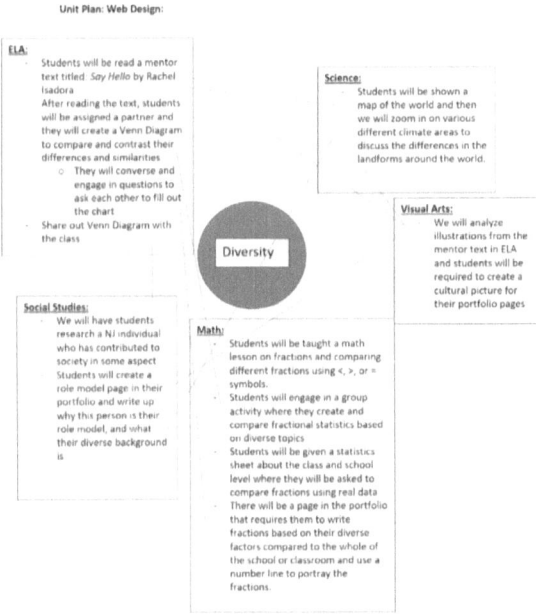

Figure 2.1. Student's Web Design of Unit Plan about "Diversity." *Image created by the authors.*

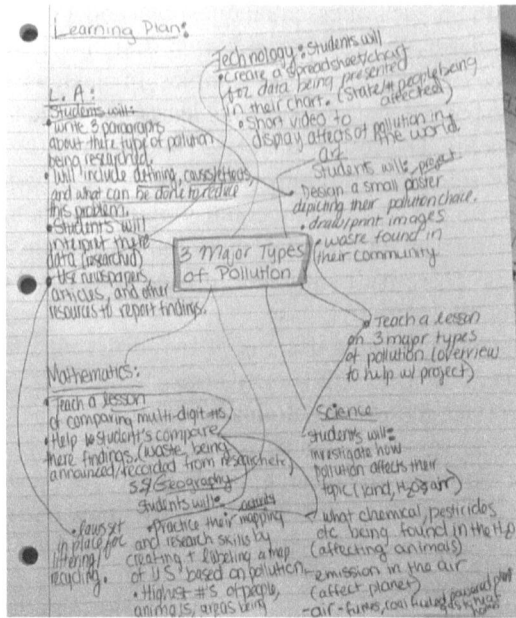

Figure 2.2. Student's Web Design of Unit Plan about "Pollution." *Image created by the authors.*

how the different web designs can look and how each gives a very good idea of what will be the focus, the connections between the disciplines, and the standards to be used. During the rest of the class session, the readings on completed unit plans are discussed. A major focus is on procedure and the assessment plans. After the discussion, students are again paired up for a workshop on their unit plans. Here they have the chance to discuss what they are thinking about doing, getting feedback if others think it will work, and begin creating their plans. We continue this workshop the following week, with students having more ideas and able to get specific feedback on their lessons. One thing that is consistently mentioned by students in our evaluations is the student's future plan to use web design in lesson planning. They state it organizes their lessons and shows clearly the standards they will teach.

Phase 4: Unit Plan Presentations

Over the last two classes, students prepare to first give an overview of their fully developed lesson plans. Here they are able to show how the essential questions and web design brought the individual lessons together. Along with this, they can discuss the ways of assessment and differentiated learning.

After this portion, the students proceed to give a short demonstration of one part of their three lessons that make up the unit plan. The demonstration is given as if it is being done in a classroom of the chosen grade.

LEARNING EXPERIENCES IN INTERDISCIPLINARY TEACHER EDUCATION

In this capstone course, ISEE major students complete surveys, discussions, and reflection papers, in addition to their course assignments such as unit projects and numerous reading responses. The data that we collected from the past four years' courses show that this interdisciplinary program and capstone course provide teacher candidates with openness and confidence in all subjects and help them develop skills to design theme-based unit plans. As future generalist elementary school teachers, students think interdisciplinary teacher education makes sense and works great for teaching all subjects in a meaningful way for students' learning.

The topics that the students chose indicate that what speakers and instructors introduced in the course greatly affected students' awareness of and interests in social justice and global sustainability issues from multiple perspectives. Many students were not confident about teaching the topics but became a lot more comfortable after this course. Some looked forward to continuing research and building their knowledge on the topics to bring into their future lessons.

Teacher candidates' knowledge and skills in interdisciplinary teaching have clearly increased. First, the students reported having knowledge of what the interdisciplinary teaching method is before starting the class. The students also reported that at the end of the semester they felt comfortable with the interdisciplinary teaching method and believed they would be able to implement it in their future classrooms. However, some students also concerned that theadministrators may not understand or want the method used.

Additionally, a few students mentioned the use of web design in future lesson planning, as it helped organize what they would do and show the standards they will teach. A few students also mentioned that they would like an easier way (recipe) to create social justice or UN sustainability lesson plans.

CONCLUSION

This chapter has highlighted a specific elementary teacher program, its outcomes on the Praxis, and the capstone in the major, which teaches the interdisciplinary method. The information, in total, shows how a university major designed to give preservice students a deep knowledge of content brings high success on the Praxis exam and provides a natural fit for the final capstone course teaching the interdisciplinary method. The hope is that more schools will adopt this major in some form, but it is not required if your school wishes to teach the interdisciplinary method. The course described above would function as a stand-alone methods course, albeit lacking in student preparation.

NOTE

1. Examples of universities that require multi-subject majors are Monmouth University, James Madison University, Virginia Commonwealth University, the University of Michigan, the University of Northern Colorado, and the University of North Texas. Virginia and Michigan are two states that have recognized that future elementary teachers need a college curriculum with breadth and depth across many subject areas in order to be effective in their own future classrooms.

REFERENCES

Brenner, D., & McQuirk, A. (2019). A snapshot of writing in elementary teacher preparation programs. *The New Educator, 15*(1), 18–29.

Fonseca, K., Maseko, J., & Roberts, N. (2018). Students' mathematical knowledge in a Bachelor of Education (foundation or intermediate phase) program. In Govender, R. & Junqueira, K. (Eds.), *Proceedings of the 24th Annual National Congress of the Association for Mathematics Education of South Africa* (pp. 124–139). University of the Free State, Bloemfontein Campus.

Greenberg, J., McKee, A., & Walsh, K. (2013). *Teacher prep review: A review of the nation's teacher preparation programs 2013*. Washington, D.C.: National Council on Teacher Quality.

Mimbs, J. C. (2002). *Geography education requirements in K–8 preservice teacher training at southern regional education board colleges and universities and development of a field-oriented model curriculum* (Order No. 3054129). [Doctoral dissertation, University of Tennessee, Knoxville]. ProQuest Dissertations and Theses Global.

Morris, A. K., & Hiebert, J. (2017). Effects of teacher preparation courses: Do graduates use what they learned to plan mathematics lessons? *American Educational Research Journal, 54*(3), 524–567.

National Board for Professional Teaching Standards. (2012a). *Middle childhood generalist standards for teachers of students ages 7–12* (3rd ed.). Arlington, VA: National Board for Professional Teaching Standards.

National Board for Professional Teaching Standards. (2012b). *Early childhood generalist standards for teachers of students ages 3–10* (3rd ed.). Arlington, VA: National Board for Professional Teaching Standards.

Passe, J. (2006). New challenges in elementary social studies. *The Social Studies*, *97*(5), 189–192.

Rech, J., Hartzell, J., & Stephens, L. (1993). Comparisons of mathematical competencies and attitudes of elementary education majors with established norms of a general college population. *School Science and Mathematics*, *93*(3), 141–144.

Trygstad, P. J. (2013). *2012 National Survey of Science and Mathematics Education: Status of elementary school science.* Chapel Hill, NC: Horizon Research, Inc.

Womac, P. (2014). The unfortunate status of geography in elementary teacher education: A call for discourse. *Research in Geographic Education*, *16*(2), 46–60.

Wood, K. (2015). *Interdisciplinary instruction, unit and lesson planning strategies K–8* (5th ed). Long Grove, IL: Waveland Press, Inc.

Chapter 3

Planning an Elementary Interdisciplinary Unit

Christine Grabowski

Elementary interdisciplinary units provide an optimal use of instructional time and deliver that instruction in a manner that is engaging and interesting to students. There are multiple approaches to planning an elementary interdisciplinary unit. Educators need to start the process by examining the curriculum and standards that are required for the grade level. Being familiar with the areas of study will aid in the brainstorming process and allow for openness to different ideas in connecting the topics.

The use of a graphic organizer for the initial planning stages is the most effective method of planning. The first type is a theme organizer as shown in figure 3.1. It has sections for each of the disciplines that can be included in the theme unit. First, determining the theme of the unit is the initial step taken in this planning process. By looking at the different instructional areas, educators can consider the kinds of activities that could be incorporated into the theme. This type of tool provides organization to the brainstorming process and creates a visual representation to assist in creating the themed unit. Any ideas of texts, topics, and materials can all be added to the organizer as a first step in the planning process.

Another tool that can be utilized is a template that is more detailed in nature (see figure 3.2). This was inspired by the Understanding by Design model developed by Grant Wiggins and Jay McTighe, which has also been referred to as "Backward Design." The designer looks at the outcomes first, and then works backward in the planning of the teaching unit. There are areas to list the standards, acceptable assessments, technology, and resources. In the planning process, there are sections to include inquiry-based statements, essential questions, cross-curricular standards, and key dispositions and knowledge. These tools provide the educator with a launching point for planning an interdisciplinary unit.

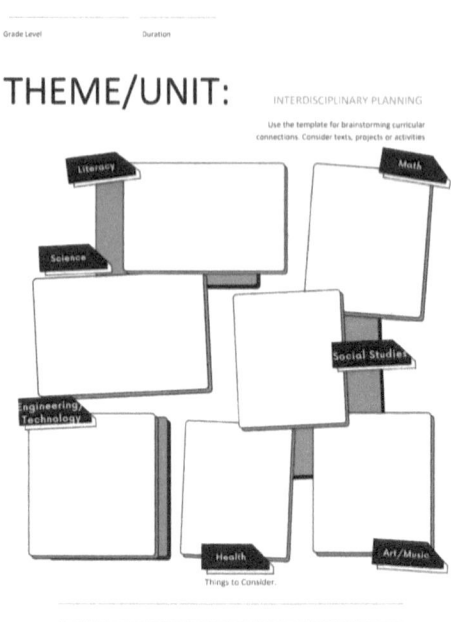

Figure 3.1. Theme/Unit Interdisciplinary Planning. *Christine Grabowski (2021).*

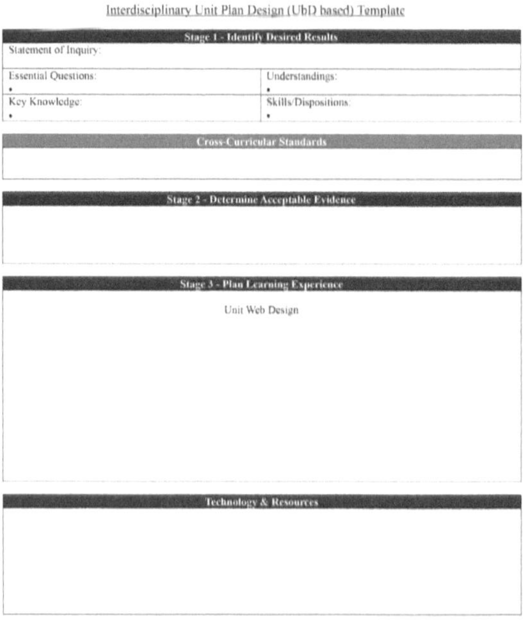
Interdisciplinary Unit Plan Design (UbD based) Template

Stage 1 - Identify Desired Results	
Statement of Inquiry:	
Essential Questions: •	Understandings: •
Key Knowledge: •	Skills/Dispositions: •

Cross-Curricular Standards

Stage 2 - Determine Acceptable Evidence

Stage 3 - Plan Learning Experience
Unit Web Design

Technology & Resources

Figure 3.2. Interdisciplinary Unit Plan Design (UbD Based) Template. *Jiwon Kim (2021), revised from Wiggins & McTighe (2005) Understanding by Design and Wood (2015) Web Design.*

The following section will outline the planning process for an elementary interdisciplinary unit, with actual examples of unit plans.

EXAMPLE 1: LIGHTHOUSES UNIT

This unit was planned for third and fourth grades, with the unit theme centered around lighthouses. First, ideas were added to the theme organizer based on the standards for third and fourth grade. The brainstorming process continued through research about books, topics, and standards. This allows the planner to be creative and recognize the links and connections that are naturally present.

Looking at literature first can be a great springboard for ways to tie in concepts. For the lighthouse unit, *The Lighthouse Keeper Series* by Ronda Armitage was selected for English Language Arts. It is a collection of eight fiction books with the same characters and their different adventures at the lighthouse. The students were placed in small groups with one of the stories and tasked with reading the book, summarizing it, and creating a presentation to share with the class.

To incorporate technology, the groups of students used the DoInk app and a green screen to share the summaries of the lighthouse stories with the whole class. Green screens allow pictures and videos to be incorporated into the background with recordings of live action. The children used their creativity to make props, choose backgrounds, and costume parts to effectively present their summary of the story. They added photos and graphics interchange format (GIF) to the app to create their story. Figure 3.3 shows the students standing in front of the green screen as they record their content. An example of a scene from the final video recording inside the lighthouse is shown in figure 3.4. This activity was highly engaging for the students as they used literacy skills simultaneously with technology.

Social studies is incorporated with another text, *The Little Red Lighthouse and the Great Gray Bridge* by Hildegarde H. Swift. This fictional story is about the building of the George Washington Bridge and Jeffrey's Hook Lighthouse, two landmarks on the Hudson River in New York. Discussions about the landmarks and reasons for the construction of the bridge fulfill the social studies standards. The specific literacy skill that was targeted for the text was visualizing, where students listened to the story and drew pictures based on their visualization. They added specific parts of the text with words that helped them visualize the scene as evidenced in figure 3.5.

Keep the Lights Burning, Abby by Connie Roop is a true story that takes place in Maine in 1856, in which a young girl kept the lighthouse lamps lit when her dad was unable during a storm. Science connections about weather tie in well with this piece of literature. The types of storms and erosion were

Figure 3.3. Green Screen Recording. *Christine Grabowski (2018).*

Figure 3.4. Green Screen Final Product. *Christine Grabowski (2018).*

studied alongside the book using the students' science textbook. To integrate technology with the literature, the students used Ozobots, which are codable robots, to identify an important event in the story. A graphic organizer was utilized to explain the action in the story along with the code used to correlate with the action.

Figure 3.5. **Visualizing Activity.** *Christine Grabowski (2021).*

Geography is infused into the interdisciplinary unit with research on lighthouses in the United States. Each student chose a lighthouse and dove deeply into a project that included art and writing. A research template was provided for students to use their non-fiction reading skills to learn about the dimensions, location, and history of the lighthouse. The next step was to write a non-fiction piece about the lighthouse to present to the class. They used a website called Incarnate to create a map of the lighthouse by looking at Google Maps as illustrated in figure 3.6. This enabled them to learn about geographic features and landforms to enhance their knowledge in a hands-on manner.

Additionally, in collaboration with the art teacher at the school, the students created a painting on canvas of their lighthouse based on a chosen photo. They were taught elements of painting such as dimension and shading as they painted their selected lighthouse. To incorporate the idea of civics, the students were invited to a local nursing home to present their research and artwork to some of the patients at the facility. Each student read a few key facts from their research while presenting their painting to the group of seniors. This was a great opportunity to experience civics in action and learn beyond the walls of the classroom. Figure 3.7 shows the students giving their paintings to the seniors at the facility.

Engineering challenges were incorporated into the themed unit to teach the engineering design process. The first challenge was a project that incorporated pretzel sticks and marshmallows to build a lighthouse to hold a tea light. Using the background knowledge that they gained through studying lighthouses, they were able to mimic designs to get the best result for holding the light up. Next, designing a boat to float and hold an action figure was part

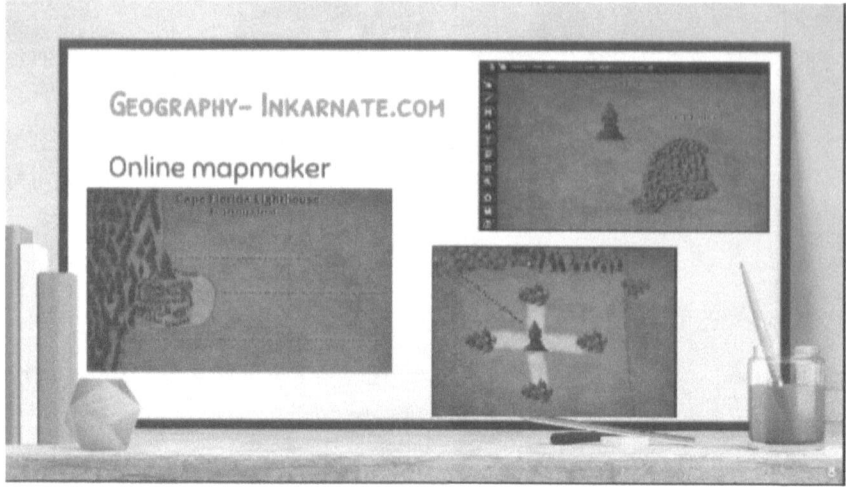

Figure 3.6. **Geography Maps Created Online.** *Christine Grabowski (2021).*

Figure 3.7. **Civics Activity.** *Christine Grabowski (2021).*

of understanding forces, buoyancy, and scientific principles. Math was incorporated into the unit along with measurement and geometry. Shapes were studied for their strength and how they apply to engineering design. Measurements were important for the specifications for each of the engineering challenges. Students used their engineering notebooks to record each step of the engineering design process, including ask, imagine, plan, create, experiment and improve. Their diagrams, charts, and graphs were all included in the notebooks to build a foundation for lab work in the future.

EXAMPLE 2: WESTWARD EXPANSION UNIT

Another example of a themed interdisciplinary unit is Westward Expansion in the United States. Each of the different subject areas can be addressed through this broad concept in a plethora of ways. The *Little House on the Prairie* series lends itself well to this concept for the literacy component and as a springboard for the teaching unit. The books by Laura Ingalls Wilder chronicle the covered wagon travels and family adventures of the Ingalls family.

Planning ways to incorporate standards can often be derived from the content of the book or novel chosen as part of the unit. In this case, Wilder writes about different types of flowers and animals that are on the prairie in *Little House on the Prairie*. As an example, "The wild larkspur was blossoming pink and blue and white, birds balanced on yellow plumes of goldenrod, and butterflies were fluttering. Starry daisies lighted the shadows under the trees" (Laura Ingalls Wilder, 1953). From the text, the students took the names of the flowers encountered in the book and, in groups, researched information about them. They looked at the scientific name, location, structure, and function. Models of the types of prairie flowers were created with craft materials, and diagrams were labeled with the parts of a plant. Science standards about plants with structure and function adaptations for growth were all being taught with relevant content taken straight out of the Wilder book. Planting seeds and tracking the growth of the flowers and plants were included to provide hands-on experiences with how they grow and develop, variables that affect growth, and gave the students opportunities to work with the data. Figure 3.8 illustrates the hydroponics tower with various types of plant growth.

From a social studies perspective, the history of the Oregon Trail is a great way to teach about maps and human population patterns. Hundreds of thousands of people traveled by covered wagon in a mass migration westward, as the Ingalls family did in the book. A study about why people traveled through the rough terrain and how the trail was established allows the students to understand the concept from a historical perspective. The landmarks that are along the trail become part of a class research project. Small groups each choose a landmark, and on a shared Google Slideshow, share information about the landmark with examples shown in figure 3.9. Geography is infused with the examination of the United States map and tracing the trail across the continent. The physical geography of the terrain, plains, mountains, and waterways is mapped out with discussions about how the land affects the travel on the trail in the wagons.

The Oregon Trail computer game found online promotes problem-solving and critical thinking. The game is based on a decision-making process about travelers on the Oregon Trail. The choice of job determines the salary and

Figure 3.8. Hydroponics Tower for Growing Plants. *Christine Grabowski (2022).*

skill set, which in turn affects the ability to purchase items to take for the journey and survive on the trail. Mathematical skills are applied in calculating the budget for the purchase of items to take on the journey, such as clothing, wagon parts, food items, and ammunition for hunting. Students are adding and subtracting, as well as using estimation to decide on their purchases. While playing the game, the player needs to make choices along the way, such as resting due to the weather, extreme heat or cold, or choosing to ford a river or wait for the water level to drop. These fictional travelers can come down with diseases, which naturally lends itself to incorporating health lessons about disease and illness. Teaching how germs spread, with lessons on good health habits and hygiene are naturally integrated into the teaching unit. This motivational game brings so many facets of the curriculum together, and the students don't even realize how much they are learning.

Engineering challenges are always a beneficial and fun part of an interdisciplinary unit. The Westward Expansion unit is no exception. As figure 3.10 shows, students were tasked with creating a covered wagon that would have specific parameters. Following the engineering design process, they used the classroom makerspace, which is an area that contains a variety of craft-like objects. The children chose materials to design and build a covered wagon that was required to roll forward and backward, have an area for an action figure to sit inside, and have a covering. There were constraints with

Planning an Elementary Interdisciplinary Unit 33

Figure 3.9. Oregon Trail Research Project. *Christine Grabowski (2021).*

regard to the size and function of the covered wagon. Students honed their mathematical skills with measurement to ensure that the covered wagon met the required criteria. Testing of the covered wagons as a group is always a highly motivating activity when students create the "wagon train" with their own engineered creations.

Language arts literacy skills are incorporated into the thematic unit easily with literature, both fiction and non-fiction. *Dandelions* by Eve Bunting is the fictional story of a family traveling west in a covered wagon. To teach the skill of compare and contrast, the children completed a Venn diagram to compare the story with *Little House on the Prairie*. With the graphic organizer, they completed a writing assignment demonstrating their understanding of comparing and contrasting two different texts. Another fictional novel that would lend itself well to this activity is *Ranger in Time Rescue on the Oregon Trail* by Kate Messner. It is the story of a golden retriever who meets a young boy and his family as they are traveling on the Oregon Trail. Reading comprehension skills with these fictional texts can be taught in a multitude of ways. Summarizing, plotting, asking questions, making predictions . . . the possibilities are endless for good-quality literacy instruction.

Informational texts are another key piece in language arts literacy. There is a book series called "If you . . ." that addresses all different topics, and two of the books are perfect for this teaching unit. *If You Were*

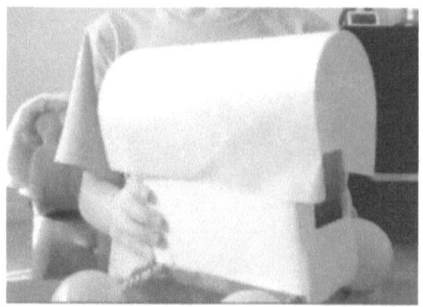

Figure 3.10. Engineering a Covered Wagon. *Christine Grabowski (2021).*

a Pioneer on the Prairie by Anne Kamma and *If You Traveled West in a Covered Wagon* by Ellen Levine both provide a question and answer format to teach about pioneer life. As read aloud, these texts spark engaging conversations and help to provide depth of knowledge on the subject matter. Finally, *You Wouldn't Want to Be an American Pioneer!: A Wilderness You'd Rather Not Tame* by Jacqueline Morley, is a picture book that teaches about pioneer life in a humorous way. Writing skills are developed through multiple activities throughout the teaching unit. Journal entries are written as the students are asked to imagine themselves as if they were pioneers traveling on the Oregon Trail. Using the knowledge that they have gathered through the read-alouds, picture books, and novels read, they write daily entries with the final activity of creating an old-fashioned cover for the journal.

Assessment of the students' knowledge on the subject matter can be ascertained through many different activities. Journal entries require certain elements of both content and mechanics and can be scored on a rubric. Reading comprehension skills are measured through activities, readers' notebook entries, and through teacher conferences with individual students. Science and social studies assessments are achieved through projects such as diagramming a flower and research projects.

EXAMPLE 3: ODYSSEY OF THE MIND

There are a myriad of themes that can become the center of an interdisciplinary unit. The educator who is planning needs to be open and think creatively about connections. There is a program that truly exudes the tenets of interdisciplinary learning and creativity. Odyssey of the Mind is a creative problem-solving competition for students in kindergarten through college. Students form teams of seven to tackle one of the five challenges offered. There is an area of focus for each of the five problems: problem one involves building vehicles, the next has a technical challenge, problem three is called "Classics" and involves art, literature, and so on. Finally, problem four includes building balsa wood structures engineered to hold as much weight as possible, and problem five is creative with a strictly performance aspect. Problem four is illustrated in figure 3.11 with two team members finalizing their structures for competition. An example of the vehicle problem with team members operating the team-built vehicle in the performance area with the rest of the team is displayed in figure 3.12.

There is a clear set of rules that need to be followed, including a budget, a time limit of eight minutes to present a solution, and required paperwork to be submitted. Teams are required to write a script, design and build scenery,

Figure 3.11. Building Balsa Wood Structures in Odyssey of the Mind. *Christine Grabowski (2022).*

Figure 3.12. Vehicle Designed and Built by Students for Odyssey of the Mind. *Christine Grabowski (2018).*

Figure 3.13. Example of Costumes and Scenery Created by an Odyssey of the Mind Team. *Christine Grabowski (2022).*

and create costumes as part of the solution. A photograph of team-created costumes for a Colonial American theme is shown in figure 3.13. Students are honing skills in writing, science and engineering, speaking and listening, and mathematics, with a list of possibilities that are endless. The teacher is considered a coach, only a supportive guide with the students taking ownership of the solution that they present to the judges. The students are developing critical skills in creative problem-solving, utilizing all subject areas while creating their solution. Odyssey of the Mind has been incorporated into classroom instruction, as well as presented as an extracurricular activity. The interdisciplinary nature of the design of the program makes it a valuable experience and way to deliver curriculum to students in a fun and meaningful manner.

YOU CAN DO IT

The curriculum is clearly integrated into the thematic teaching units presented. It is always interesting to observe students who are just immersed in their learning and have no clear delineation of when they are learning each specific subject. The integration throughout the activities allows the learners to absorb knowledge in a natural manner. So often, schedules are created with blocks of time dedicated to each subject, and teachers feel compelled to stop, close a text, and move on to the next subject. With thematic interdisciplinary units, there is a natural progression and integration that is seamless. The learning is deep and meaningful to the students because of how invested they are in the activities. Interdisciplinary teaching units at the elementary level are the perfect way to grasp the interest and attention of students and provide them with knowledge that has substantial depth and breadth. Educators need to be creative and open to thinking outside the box when planning and implementing these types of units. The result will be classes of students who are ready to take on their own education and the world!

REFERENCES

Armitage, R., & Armitage, D. (2008). *The Lighthouse Keeper Stories*. London: Scholastic.
Bunting, E. (2001). *Dandelions*. Logan, IA: Perfection Learning.
Incarnate.com. (2023). http://incarnate.com
Kamma, A., & Watling, J. (2006). *If You Were a Pioneer on the Prairie*. New York: Scholastic.
Levine, E., & Freem, E. (2006). *If You Traveled West in a Covered Wagon*. New York: Scholastic.
Messner, K. (2015). *Rescue on the Oregon Trail (Ranger in Time #1)*. New York: Scholastic Inc.
Morley, J., & Antram, D. (2013). *You Wouldn't Want to Be an American Pioneer!: A Wilderness You'd Rather Not Tame*. New York: Franklin Watts.

"Odyssey of the Mind—the Peak of beyond the Box Thinking." (n.d.). www.odysseyofthemind.com. Retrieved May 16, 2023. http://odysseyofthemind.com

"The Oregon Trail." (2018). ClassicReload.com. December 12, 2018. https://classicreload.com/oregon-trail.html

Roop, P., & Roop, C. (2018). *Keep the Lights Burning, Abbie*. Minneapolis, MN: Lerner Publishing Group.

Swift, H. H., Ward, L., Terheyden, J., & Live. (1970). *The Little Red Lighthouse and the Great Gray Bridge*. San Diego: Harcourt, Inc.

Wiggins, G. P., & McTighe, J. (2005). *Understanding by Design*. 2nd ed. Upper Saddle River, NJ: Pearson.

Wilder, L. I. (1953). *Little House on the Prairie*. New York: Scholastic Incorporated.

Chapter 4

Interdisciplinary Instruction Supports Thinking and Writing

Hank Bitten

Everyone talks about the value of interdisciplinary education, but only a few teachers and districts are doing it effectively. There are many pressures on elementary teachers to teach writing and literacy, differentiate instruction, teach inquiry-based lessons, integrate technology, and prepare their students for state assessments. Teachers are also held accountable for implementing the content standards in their state.

According to Allen Repko, director of the Interdisciplinary Studies program at the University of Texas in Arlington, teachers of the humanities claim significant learning gains in critical thinking:

> This collective claim to critical thinking raises the question: How do interdisciplinary approaches contribute to the development of this key cognitive skill in ways that are different from or superior to single-subject approaches? "For a learner to be truly empowered through critical thinking," says Toynton (2005),"more than one context or one discipline needs to be encountered." (Repko, 2008, p. 172)

Interdisciplinary instruction provides a perspective on the disciplinary concepts that are part of each discipline, and these connections help students with the process of learning. When students make connections between similar content across disciplines (i.e., weather, climate, or civics and examples in literature, math, and science) and with real-world connections (the causes and solutions of climate change), they benefit from a wide perspective of how each discipline uses evidence and approaches a problem.

Unfortunately, there are barriers that interfere with interdisciplinary education at every level in the structure of education. There is limited time for planning interdisciplinary lessons, preservice education courses do not address interdisciplinary education adequately, there is confusion between intradisciplinary and interdisciplinary education, and there are distractions within the daily school schedule. As a result, teachers often substitute interdisciplinary education for interdisciplinary connections.

In *The Big Short*, Harry Stein states that "American students are in school for thirteen disconnected years. In grades K–5 students learn in a reading/language arts/mathematics skill-based school. Most students have one classroom teacher" (2020, p. 1). This structure does not support experiences for students to understand the argument, the evidence, the process of investigating, strategies for analyzing problems, and debating possible solutions. The "Big Short" is when instruction does not translate into lasting memory and is quickly forgotten because thinking is omitted from instruction.

In *Unlearning the Ropes* (2022), Denise Bressler supports the evidence from the study at the Jet Propulsion Laboratory that education needs to involve structured and free play because these experiences provide children with an opportunity to be passionate about what they are learning:

> According to Stuart Brown, starting in the late 1990s, Cal Tech's Jet Propulsion Laboratory started noticing that young hires were not as good at problem solving and innovative thinking as older engineers. The managers who noticed the phenomenon were perplexed. It seemed so strange, because they were hiring graduates from top universities such as MIT and Stanford—so why were their thinking skills subpar? The Jet Propulsion Laboratory investigated the problem and made an interesting discovery: the younger generation had not experienced hands-on play as children. Employees who had played with their hands as children were simply better at seeing solutions to problems; those without such childhood play struggled. Essentially, students who succeed academically are generally not the creative thinkers or innovative doers that we need. Managers were so convinced of the connection that they actually changed their interview process to ask potential hires about their childhood play experiences. (p. 124)

Interdisciplinary learning is not free play; it is structured play! It provides differentiated connections that engage students in their learning by providing an environment for activities that are enjoyable and memorable. The examples in this chapter will focus on exemplary cases from the K–5 social studies curriculum in different school districts.

STANDARDS MODEL

Our first example is a Standards Model enabling students to understand their responsibilities as global citizens. The examples are from the curriculum at a suburban district in Bergen County, New Jersey for grades K–2. The critical content for students in grade 1 involves studying the environment, climate change, and the use of natural resources. Students are asked to find evidence of natural resources and renewable and nonrenewable sources of energy. In addition to understanding the importance of natural resources to sustaining life, students make connections to how supply and demand influence prices and the local, national, and global economy (Grade 1 Citizenship Unit).

The interdisciplinary framework aligns standards from various disciplines, especially English Language Arts, Social Studies, Science, and the Arts. The Learning Standards provide direct connections for an interdisciplinary model of instruction. Using their online curriculum, let's examine the core content for grade 1 from the perspectives of social studies and English Language Arts. In the Learning Standards below (see table 4.1), note the disciplinary concepts of civic-mindedness, geography, economic thinking, and interactions with the local community. The study of climate change drives the connection for related content in other disciplines.

An effective strategy for expanding from intradisciplinary to interdisciplinary planning is to provide learning activities that support student research, exploration, and problem-solving within the performance expectations of the subject matter in the curriculum. Consider figure 4.1 regarding climate change, which begins with identifying the problem with relevance to the student's experience.

Table 4.1. An Intradisciplinary Planner for Studying the Environment in Grades K–2.

Climate	Civics	Economics
Investigate a global issue such as climate change, its significance, and share information about how it impacts different regions around the world	Use examples from a variety of sources to describe how certain characteristics can help individuals collaborate and solve problems	Identify examples of human capital, physical capital, and natural resources that contribute to favorable economic conditions
Explain how seasonal weather changes, climate, and other environmental characteristics affect people's lives in a place or region	Describe why it is important that individuals assume personal and civic responsibilities in a democratic society	Describe the goods and services that individuals and businesses in the local community might use to reduce carbon
Describe how human activities affect the culture and environmental characteristics of places or regions	Make a presentation to elected leaders about the harms of our local carbon footprint	Describe how supply and demand influence the price and output of products when there is a shortage due to extreme weather

Step 1: Identifying the Problem—individual behaviors and actions affect our climate.

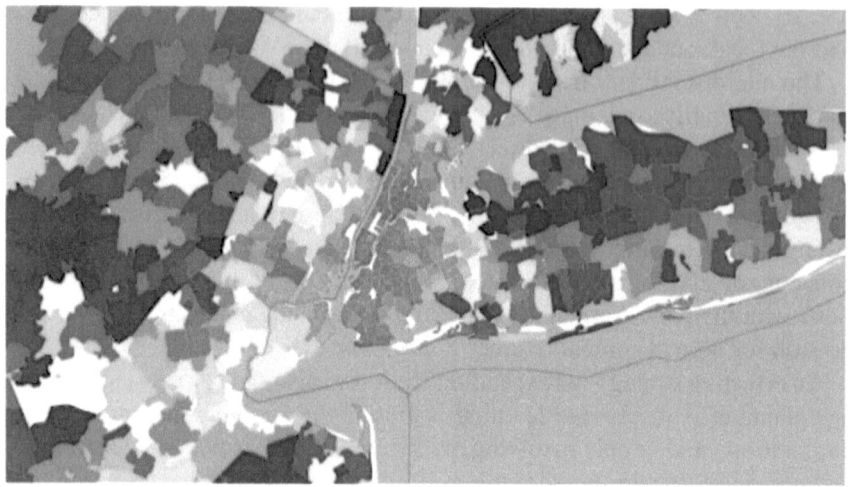

Figure 4.1. My Carbon Footprint. *basf.com.*

Why is the carbon footprint for emissions higher in the suburbs than in urban areas?

Step 2: Impact Beyond My Community—our actions as a school and community have a larger impact. (See figure 4.2.)

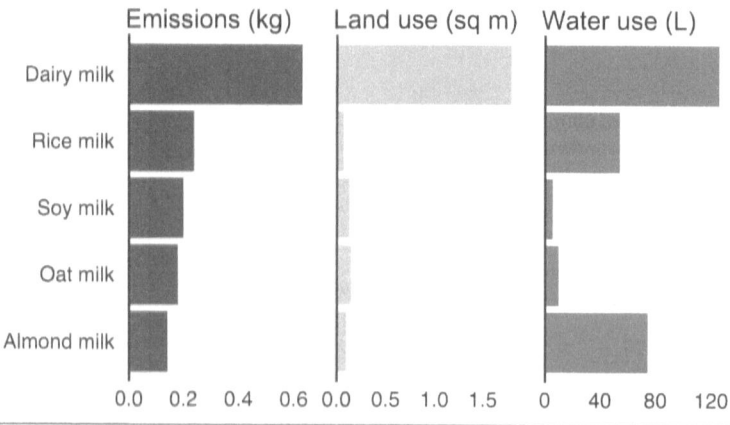

Figure 4.2. How Does My Diet Affect the Environment and Climate? *Poore & Nemecek (2018), Science. Additional calculations, J. Poore.*

Step 3: Economic Costs—the effects of global warming and climate change are costly. (See figure 4.3.)

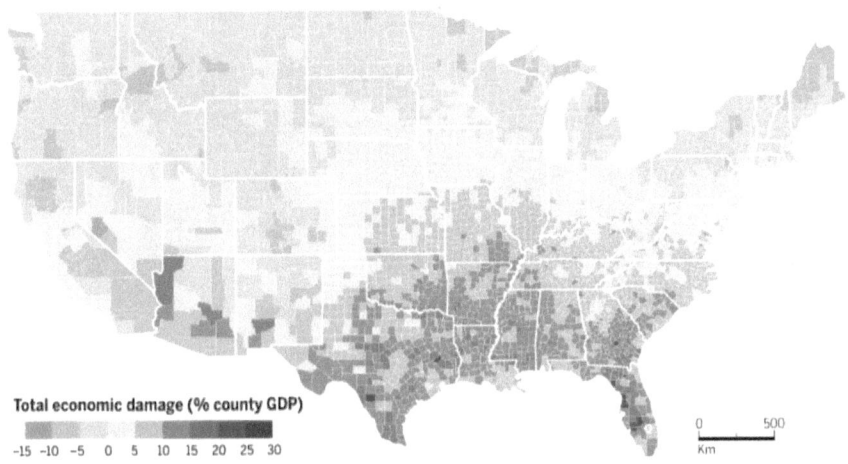

Figure 4.3. What Are the Likely Causes for the Economic Costs from Climate and Environmental Changes? (Flooding, Hurricanes, Drought, Wildfires, Early Freezes, Severe Storms). *Hsiang et al., adapted by G. Grullon/Science.*

Step 4: Solutions—there are decisions we can take to reduce the impact of costly climate change effects. (See figure 4.4.)

Figure 4.4. Alternatives to Using Carbon-Free Energy. *(Left) Unknown. (Center) Bengt Halvorsen (2022). (Right) GettyImages (2012).*

Step 5: Civic Engagement—through decision-making, we take constructive action to protect the environment. (See figure 4.5.)

Figure 4.5. Classroom Debate. *https://dlesfifthgrade.weebly.com/team-5-blog/busy-as-can-be.*

Using the Standards Model, students can participate in problem-solving and decision-making learning activities that connect learning to memory. The bridge between literacy and memory involves making connections with real-world and practical examples. Climate education is one example that supports interdisciplinary learning. The view in table 4.2 provides clarity on what students with differentiated abilities should be learning in their social studies, math, science, and technology classes.

Table 4.2. Example of Differentiated Learning Activities Based on Learning Styles.

	Visual	Kinesthetic	Inquiry
Group A	Analyze Temperature Maps and compare changes over time	Diagram or build a solar energy panel	Research how carbon emissions influence climate over time
Group B	Analyze Precipitation Maps and compare changes over time	Produce a collage or video of windmills	Research the costs of solar and wind energy as compared to carbon-based fuels
Group C	Study images of melting ice caps and glaciers	Publish an informational graphic on resources for green energy	Research costs and savings of green energy for a home or school

Before examining the connections with English Language Arts, let's focus on the primary skills defined in the curriculum for grade 1 students. The skills are presented in three categories supporting the core content:

A. Understanding what global means and how all of the people of the world are connected.
   To identify the characteristics of a global citizen.
   Identifying global citizens who have had an impact on our world.

B. To understand how climate change and overuse are depleting natural resources.

C. Identifying goods, services, and natural resources.
   Understanding that as the supply and demand for goods and services change, so does the price.
   Identify renewable and nonrenewable resources.

These skills scaffold the critical content outlined above in social studies with English Language Arts. First, it is important to provide resources relating to the concept of "global" and "good citizens." Second, it is important to understand the concept of scarcity and the depletion of natural resources, especially ice, water, and trees. Third, it is important for young students to articulate their understanding of supply and demand and how warmer temperatures will affect the price of food and water or the cost to repair damage from severe weather. Through an interdisciplinary approach, student learning is enhanced through carefully planned connections and the analysis of different perspectives in the English Language Arts curriculum.

The Learning Standards for English Language Arts support the core content and skills in the social studies curriculum. The example that follows is from the Tenafly Public Schools in New Jersey and is an effective model for interdisciplinary instruction.

A. Knowledge and Ideas

(The Learning Standards in table 4.3 are restated concisely for the purpose of illustration. Visit the Tenafly Public Schools website for ELA Standards.)

Depending on the strategies for differentiated learning, student learning with an intentional interdisciplinary design will follow one of the following engaging activities.

Table 4.3. Interdisciplinary Connections for Grade 1.

ELA Learning Standard	Social Studies Connection	Interdisciplinary Skills	Interdisciplinary Connections
Integrate knowledge visually	Illustrate carbon footprint	Connection to how human activities change environments	Social Studies, ELA, Art
Use illustrations to support content	Images of droughts, floods, and storm damage	Connection to the supply and demand of goods and services	Social Studies, ELA, Art
Evaluate the claim or argument	Provide evidence that climate is changing as a result of human activity	Identifying a claim	Social Studies, ELA
Identify reasons for the author's perspective	Examples from literature (i.e., a children's book *Still Waiting* by Danielle Lee)	Understanding perspectives	Social Studies, ELA
Analyze two or more sources	Images from a children's book *Still Waiting* and video sources	Researching credible sources	Social Studies, ELA
Identify similarities and differences in text and sources	Venn diagram of similarities and differences	Academic literacy	Social Studies, ELA

B. Close Reading

- Asking and answering questions about the environment and climate
- Determining the main idea or purpose of the literature
- Understanding perspectives and point of view
- Analyzing the structure of the reading
- Comparing information in text and images.

C. Writing

- Use evidence to support a claim or argument
- Gather and organize relevant information
- Determine the credibility of information
- Write an opinion or point of view.

D. Speaking, Listening, and Presentation

- Decide on a forum for collaborative conversations or presentation
- Ask questions, engage in cross examination to determine accuracy of the conversation
- Evaluate the evidence
- Present a solution or action plan
- Provide a summary and clarify the main points of each speaker.

In this model, there are significant opportunities for developing academic literacy and memory independent of the content in textbooks. The Standards Model uses content from digital media, stories, and supplemental materials. The teaching of perspectives, points of view, inquiry, research, speaking and debating, and the elements of writing are the foundations for academic literacy, thinking, and memory that endures. The capstone for interdisciplinary learning in this example for grade 1 is the critical content about a changing environment and climate. The strategies and resources provide the knowledge for making connections between the student and their experiences in the world. The coordinated effort of researching the reasons for a changing environment, proposing solutions, evaluating literature, reflecting diverse perspectives, and preparing a presentation to an audience of decision-makers becomes a meaningful learning experience for young students. The teacher becomes the chef who carefully selects the choices for a nutritional educational dinner!

ASSESSMENT MODEL

The second example is an assessment model and the online examples for grades 3–5 in a large district in Camden County, New Jersey. The example selected is for a unit on teaching the geography of New Jersey. (Grade 3 Humanities)

The two essential questions for student inquiry are:

1. How does geography affect the way we live?
2. How can maps and charts help settlers, farmers, business people, and tourists learn valuable information to make decisions?

The study of state and local geography and history allows teachers to identify inquiry-based resources that develop skills, emphasize the development of government, culture, and economy over time, and connect students with their community, state, and region. Although lesson objectives for geography, civics, or economics may at first appear to be limited to social studies, the curriculum provides connections with what is also being taught in grades 3–5 in other disciplines. The examples of interdisciplinary assessments below are driven by the Learning Standards for learning about state history, in this case New Jersey, with instructional activities or assessments in other disciplines.

Teachers focus their teaching in the context of their own discipline about New Jersey but the assessments are designed to measure similar outcomes across different subject areas. Instead of taking one bite of vegetables, meat, and pasta at a time, students eat their vegetables first, then their meat, and the pasta later. The nutritional value is not compromised. Here is an example from social studies for a lesson on the contributions of people from New Jersey and their connections with art, music, science, and English Language Arts:

Social Studies—6.1.5. Civics CM.5 Investigate the lives of New Jersey individuals with diverse experiences who have contributed to the improvement of society. Using an assessment model, students in art could analyze cartoon drawings of New Jersey artists in the context of the skills and learning objectives in the curriculum. For example, *Caspar the Ghost and Felix the Cat* by Joseph Oriolo (Woodcliff Lake, New Jersey) and *Uncle Wiggily Longears* by Howard Garis (Newark, New Jersey). Students in music might research the lyrics to "American the Beautiful" or find connections to New Jersey using the music of Dionne Warwick, Bruce Springsteen, or others.

Interdisciplinary connections in science can be taught independently with students understanding cause and effect relationships, the contributions of scientists and engineers, and the places in New Jersey where they originated. Examples include Hellmann's Mayonnaise (Englewood Cliffs), Trident gum (Morris Plains), and Carrier Air Conditioning (Newark).

In English Language Arts, students can read biographies of people from New Jersey who have made a difference or a significant contribution. For example, Gen. Hugh Mercer, Albert Einstein, George Merck, Carl Lewis, Larry Doby, Yogi Berra, Joe Theismann, Paul Robeson, and Frank Sinatra are appropriate individuals for children in grades 3–5.

The assessment model does not require extensive teacher planning or that the units be taught at the same time. The advantage is the flexibility that enables students to learn social studies through the lens of different disciplines. The curriculum provides the content, and the teachers provide the connections through their formative assessments.

Below is an example relating to three Learning Standards for the geography of New Jersey, which provides interdisciplinary connections through assessments:

6.1.5.EconEM.4   Compare different regions of New Jersey to determine the role that geography, natural resources, climate, transportation, technology, and/or the labor force play in economic opportunities.

6.1.5.EconNM.2   Use data to describe how the availability of resources in New Jersey and other regions in the United States have impacted economic opportunities.

6.1.5.EconNM.3   Describe how the development of different transportation systems impacted the economies of New Jersey and the United States.

These three examples of similar content relating to concepts in economics can be taught using content examples from colonial America, the nineteenth century, and/or current examples. In a math class, students can calculate the distances between two or more places using aerial and road maps. In teaching about canals, students in math can calculate the angles of inclined planes used in the construction of canals. In English Language Arts, they can read stories about canals, railroads, bridges, and tunnels. The science unit about human activity provides an opportunity for studying cause and effect examples relating to transportation, work, and long-range impacts on climate.

UNIT MODEL

A third example is from the Unit on Economics and Financial Literacy for grades 3–5. Assessments in the areas of Social Studies/Economics and Financial Literacy can be visualized in the differentiated assessment model that follows.

Table 4.4 provides interdisciplinary connections on taxes to the local school where students attend, their home, and the community. It also provides an opportunity to develop their skills in math by making calculations to predict the impact of a tax decrease or increase. In English Language Arts, students are connected with news articles reflecting different points of view and proposing solutions to elected or appointed leaders. The assessment model allows students to learn the concepts and skills in the content of specific disciplines with examples relating to social studies. Coordination and collaboration are necessary for implementation.

Table 4.4. Interdisciplinary Unit in Teaching Economics and Financial Literacy.

Learning Standard	Social Studies: Economics and Financial Literacy	Math	English Language Arts
9.1.5.EG.1: Explain and give examples of what is meant by the term "tax"	Explain how schools are funded	Calculate a 2 percent increase in the taxes of a home in your community	Read two or more news articles on local taxes and compare the different points of view
9.1.5.EG.2: Describe how tax monies are spent	Explain how schools distribute money back to the community	Make a spreadsheet to illustrate how schools spend money	Make a budget presentation regarding the importance of education
9.1.5.EG.3: Explain the impact of the economic system on one's personal financial goals	Explain how an increase or decrease in taxes affects the budget and financial plans of people and households	Calculate and make a prediction of the impact a 4 percent change in income taxes will have on the budget of people or households with three different incomes	Write a letter to a local government leader regarding an increase or decrease in taxes

Source: NJ Social Studies Learning Standards, pp. 24–26

REFERENCES

Bressler, D. M. (2022). *Unlearning the Ropes: The Benefits of Rethinking What School Teaches You*. DIO Press.

Cherry Hill Public Schools Curriculum. "Atlas—Grade 3 Humanities Curriculum (M) District Elementary / Grade 3 / Social Studies." www.rubiconatlas.org

Lee, D. (2021). *Still Waiting*. BookBaby.

New Jersey Department of Education. "Social Studies Student Learning Standards." Retrieved from https://www.nj.gov/education/standards/socst/

Repko, A. F. (Fall 2008). "Assessing Interdisciplinary Learning Outcomes." *Academic Exchange Quarterly*. Retrieved from https://interdisciplinarystudies.org/docs/syllabi/Assessing_Interdisciplinary_Learning_Outcomes_%28Allen_F._Repko%29.pdf

Stein, H. (November 2020). "The Big Short." *Teaching Social Studies*. Retrieved from https://teachingsocialstudies.org/2020/11/13/academic-literacy-defining-the-big-short/

Tenafly Public Schools Curriculum. "Atlas Citizenship." Retrieved from https://tenaflyk12-public.rubiconatlas.org/Atlas/Develop/UnitMap/View/Default?BackLink=20301&UnitID=14817&YearID=2022&CurriculumMapID=850

"Why Teach with an Interdisciplinary Approach?" *Pedagogy in Action*. May 2021. https://serc.carleton.edu/sp/library/interdisciplinary/why.html

Chapter 5

An Interdisciplinary Approach for Secondary Schools

Hank Bitten and Mark Pearcy

Early in my high school teaching career, the movie *Titanic* premiered and was an instant, massive global hit. Practically all of my students saw the film, often multiple times, and were (to put it mildly) enthusiastic in their praise. I had been interested in the story of the doomed ship for most of my life and had read nearly everything that I could find about it; given the movie's popularity and my students' obvious interest, I decided to create a unit of study based on the incident, culminating with a viewing of the film.

There were multiple days of instruction dedicated to the unit; we had activities on social class (a prominent part of both the story of *Titanic*'s sinking and the film), the U.S. reaction to immigrants on board (those that were considered "desirable"—primarily those from Western Europe—and those that were not), and ethical issues, especially whether or not survivors on half-filled lifeboats were obligated to return for passengers in the water and thus risk being swamped.

I also tried to incorporate other topics outside the social studies. We did a short activity on the freezing temperature of seawater (lower than freshwater, due to salinity), as well as the process by which air was forced out of *Titanic*'s compartments by flooding and the geometric nature of its sinking (accelerated, ironically, by the unique nature of the ship's watertight doors). Since I wasn't a science or math teacher, these activities weren't especially detailed or rigorous, but I felt they added a degree of cross-disciplinary knowledge that was valuable (if not especially well-done or well-considered).

After several years, I scrapped the unit—not due to waning interest on the students' part, but because it was a sizable time commitment in an already crowded semester, about an event that ultimately had very little real historical impact (outside of symbolism and changes in shipping requirements). But the unit represents, in many ways, the difficulty secondary educators face in developing and employing truly interdisciplinary experiences.

This is troubling, since social studies is uniquely fertile ground for such approaches. That reality can be the basis for adapting traditional method-based training to foster the skills, dispositions, and level of student engagement we all believe is possible to attain. In this chapter, we describe the challenges facing secondary educators in teaching in an interdisciplinary manner, as well as the unique opportunities social studies teachers have to do just that. Finally, we describe how teacher educators are adapting to foster those skills and dispositions in their candidates.

INTERDISCIPLINARY EDUCATION FOR CLASSROOM TEACHERS

For most teachers, interdisciplinary education is a hazy concept, given the "modern system of disciplinarity" dominating most schools, in which academic departments are separated and treated as discrete entities (Klein, 2006, p. 10). In practice, of course, most teachers cross over academic boundaries on a daily basis, crisscrossing between different disciplinary tools, concepts, and content. However, a formalized "interdisciplinary" model is less common at either the departmental or school-wide level. At the secondary level, this is mostly because teachers operate more or less independently of each other, particularly in high schools. This is in spite of the fact that research indicates that students routinely do better (and enjoy learning more) when they see the interconnectedness of different subjects (Rissinger, 2006).

It is important to distinguish, as much as is practicable, between *multidisciplinary* education and *interdisciplinary* education. The former may be termed more incidentally (and less intentionally) connected to major themes or ideas (Applebee, Burroughs, & Cruz, 2000), while the latter adopts a more active stance toward such themes (Burns, 2002). Interdisciplinary education, then, is an approach in which "subjects and disciplines become tools for studying a theme, a problem, a question, or an idea" (Klein, 2019, p. 15).

The role of the teacher is vital in not only promoting interdisciplinary tools and skills but also navigating the various challenges inherent in developing those approaches. The value in an interdisciplinary stance is manifest (Oberdörfer et al., 2021); paradoxically, though, as teachers gain experience, they may also become less willing to adapt to the more thematically-oriented approach which characterizes interdisciplinary pedagogy. Teacher educators, therefore, need to help foster these attitudes with preservice teachers, to "mimic the interdisciplinary nature of the profession" which they will be joining (Thacker & Bodle, 2022, p. 1–2).

THE CHALLENGES OF INTERDISCIPLINARY APPROACHES IN SECONDARY EDUCATION

It is axiomatic that interdisciplinary education is a more natural fit in elementary schools, given the team-based pedagogical approach common to that level. In high school, interdisciplinary projects, initiatives, or pedagogy are primarily determined by individual teachers' willingness to undertake them—no one told me to create a unit based on *Titanic*, for example, just as no one suggested it or proscribed its use, at either the school or district levels. There are excellent examples of interdisciplinary teaching at the secondary level—a middle school nearby holds an annual eighth grade project rooted in climate change and social justice that employs multiple teachers across different disciplines, for instance—but such projects are harder to find in high schools, which generally employ a department-based, and not a team-based, model.

Interdisciplinary education in high school social studies faces challenges such as scheduling courses, common prep periods, the requirements of mandated learning standards, the importance of Advanced Placement (AP) exams on student transcripts, competition with electives, and the expense of supplementary readers. Administrators and teachers understand the importance of interdisciplinary models of learning because of their relevance to AP history exams, expository writing, defending claims with evidence, and developing memory.

Of course, part of this is due to teacher training. Elementary teachers are generalists who have to teach a wide variety of topics and disciplines, but at a relatively low level of disciplinary expertise (while a fourth grade teacher definitely includes science as a topic in their classroom, no one would reasonably expect that teacher to have mastered, for instance, upper-level physics). Secondary education majors are typically taught by content-area experts (historians, chemists, and the like) and consequently can have a more sophisticated base of content knowledge, while simultaneously having a limited grasp of different subjects that may encourage them to develop interdisciplinary lessons.

In field placements and student teaching experiences, secondary education candidates are placed with mentor teachers who are responsible for several different "preps," which can give the preservice educator the opportunity to teach different topics—but they are rarely truly disparate experiences. A chemistry teacher might be responsible for both introductory-level chemistry and advanced chemistry, but there is little variation beyond that. This is not to dismiss the difficulty of those subjects, or the challenges of teaching at different levels, but the specialization inherent in secondary education, reflected in preservice field components, is another limitation on true interdisciplinary teaching.

Among the traditional subject areas at the high school level, social studies might represent the best vehicle for such teaching, given its substantially more varied breadth and scope. A social studies teacher might be responsible for a U.S. history course, a World Civilizations course, and any number of different classes—sociology, psychology, geography, law studies, political science (both United States and comparative), and so forth. Since social studies is driven by a theme—the study of human behavior—across multiple dimensions (temporal, behavioral, and spatial). But while social studies may be the most promising entryway into interdisciplinary teaching at the secondary level, there are also unique challenges inherent in the field, outlined below.

THE UNIQUE NATURE OF SOCIAL STUDIES INSTRUCTION

One problem for social studies has been as chronic as it is depressing—most students, frankly, do not like it. Social studies is routinely cited by students as one of the most disliked subjects in the secondary curriculum (Wiggins, 2015), one in which students routinely feel as if they are being treated like vessels for informational knowledge rather than as scholars of the past who can contribute to the development of new knowledge (Wineburg, 1997, p. 255). The most dispiriting element of this reality is that social studies teachers know how rich and dynamic our subject *can* be, a reality that isn't only supported by our native bias—as Stodolsky, Salk, and Glaessner (1991) asserted three decades ago, social studies is unique among academic disciplines in that students' affection for it is determined by "whether or not the content was boring or interesting, rather than (as with math) if they were good or bad at it" (p. 89).

It is worth considering why social studies teachers are, among other disciplinary backgrounds, unique in their own right. Outside of the unusual number and types of duties that social studies teachers encompass in the secondary school environment, they are also distinctive for the relatively low percentage of non-traditional entry into the profession (e.g., alternative certification programs)—80 percent of educators joined the workforce after graduating from a traditional college-based four-year or five-year certification program. This is compounded by the fact that there are relatively low levels of misalignment between their academic preparation and their teaching assignments—only 7 percent, which means that over nine out of ten social studies teachers are focused on subjects for which they explicitly trained (Hansen et al., 2018, p. 38). These teachers are also committed to the profession for the long haul—almost three-quarters (73 percent) say they plan to remain in the classroom until retirement or as long as they are able, slightly more than other academic disciplines (Hansen et al., 2018, p. 34).

All of this illustrates that the foundation for effective interdisciplinary pedagogy is a comparatively strong one. This should, theoretically, empower us to find solutions in preservice teacher education. A similar situation is observable in how we conceive, philosophically, what our academic area actually means—in effect, what we mean when we say *social studies*. Practically since the beginning of public education in the United States, there has been a long-running debate between two distinct views of what aims we should have as teachers—one camp advocated the preeminence of history instruction, while the other focused on a more interdisciplinary approach termed, somewhat generically, "social studies" (Austin, 2003). The former group believed that a lack of rigor and a fading commitment to historical knowledge translated into a malaise of poor citizenship and a fragmented understanding of our nation's past, while the latter group decried the traditional emphasis on rote learning, memorization, and what often seemed to be enforced patriotism.

This dichotomy is surely false to a degree; the era of accountability described above undeniably encouraged a push among many teachers toward traditional history-based instruction over the admittedly more time-consuming, "messy" pedagogy of social studies. No social studies teacher would seriously dispute the preeminence of history in social studies, to the point that for many students (and teachers, too), the terms are essentially interchangeable (Lee, 2005, p. 61). Because, academically, *social studies* cross over so many different and distinct disciplines—anthropology, sociology, psychology, as well as United States and world history, geography, and even law studies—it often appears to lack, on its own, what Lee (2005) calls the "fungibility" or interchangeability of a traditional discipline. As he asserts,

> Given that social studies has no consistent or universal academic substance, arguments about what social studies should be are bound to be contentious. In fact, the instability of social studies has contributed to the many efforts to graft other existing disciplinary structure onto social studies. (Lee, 2005, p. 61)

In a sense, though, this lack of fungibility means that social studies (combined with the fact that the discipline is not as frequently subjected to standardized assessment as other subjects) have both a uniquely interdisciplinary character and an element of permissive adaptability that other secondary-level subjects lack. Even if history traditionally dominates what we think of as "social studies," the study of that topic necessarily requires teachers to draw on "ideas, theories, concepts, and methods of inquiry associated with many other academic disciplines."

"A DOG'S BREAKFAST": THE PRESERVICE EDUCATIONAL EXPERIENCE IN COLLEGE

The phrase "a dog's breakfast" has been used, at various times, to refer to a half-prepared mix of cast-off bits and pieces or as something revolting and/or unnecessary, but in common parlance, when used at all, it refers to a hodge-podge mix of a bit of everything, a *farrago* mix of often disparate elements (Safire, 1993). The phrase could be viewed pejoratively, but social studies teachers will recognize it as a strength of their discipline—because they can draw on so many different threads and create an interdisciplinary framework that can engage students in a surprising variety of ways.

Training preservice teachers to do this, however, can be challenging. Teacher education courses in many colleges do not include interdisciplinary strategies. It is important that teachers understand the perspectives of the disciplinary concepts of other subjects, especially literature, the fine arts, math, and science. Since most traditional teacher education programs employ a series of "methods" classes (usually field-based) as the primary platform for such training, most candidates will therefore have two or perhaps three courses in which to acquire not only the pedagogical skills and content knowledge necessary to function in a classroom but also the disposition to employ the array of social studies-themed topics at their disposal.

Consider, for example, the standard senior-level methods course I teach at Rider University—what we call SED 405, Teaching Social Studies in the Secondary School. I have taught this course every fall semester since my arrival at Rider in 2012, and it is easily the most-revised curriculum I have ever employed. This course is a single semester, typically just prior to the students' capstone teaching experience in their final term at the university. It is paired with a field placement at a local high school—in practical terms, the class meets one day a week (usually Tuesdays), with a full day in the field on Thursdays. At our university, students who wish to be social studies teachers are double majors—one major in secondary education and one in history (students *can* be certified to teach the subject with a different social studies-related major, like political science, but the vast majority of our students take history as their main subject of study). This means that, in their time at Rider, students will take between thirty-three and thirty-six credit hours in the study of history and historiography, with only a few classes on other social studies-related topics—for example, anthropology, sociology, psychology, and economics—scattered in where possible. This means that SED 405 is meant to be the site in which students not only learn to *teach* social studies but also to supplement the content knowledge they will need in case they are offered a position teaching, for instance, three classes of U.S. history and two classes of financial literacy (this leads to an only half-joking comment I employ in my class: "What do you say if a principal asks you to teach five classes of financial literacy?" You say "yes, please"—and then you learn on the job, like all of us).

It may go without saying that a course which meets only once a week, and places such a premium on the practical dimensions of a field placement, is a tenuous platform from which to accomplish this goal. This is why the course has been revised so many times, and, in line with the adaptive nature of the social studies discipline, the course has mutated over time to fit the particular needs of both the university and the profession.

But social studies teachers at the secondary level still manage to create rich and engaging opportunities for interdisciplinary education, in spite of the obstacles. In the section below, we describe a model that has incorporated multiple such opportunities with considerable success.

A CASE STUDY OF INTERDISCIPLINARY EDUCATION

The Ridgewood Public Schools in Bergen County, New Jersey, offers one example of a multidisciplinary model of education using social studies as the foundation for understanding the perspectives of other disciplines. Literature, art, and science have their own core content, and social studies offers a context for implementing policies, connecting with the experiences of ordinary people through art, music, and literature.

Ridgewood High School is located in Bergen County, New Jersey, and has more than a half century of experience with interdisciplinary studies courses using the disciplinary concepts in history, English literature, art, music, and science. They offer five courses with differentiated instruction for students in grades 10 and 11. The student population is about 1,800 students, with 425 on average in each grade. Ridgewood uses a rotating block schedule program. For example, a grade 10 interdisciplinary program might be scheduled in the morning during periods 3 and 4 and a grade 10 program in the afternoon during periods 7 and 8. This allows students to experience the interdisciplinary course in social studies and English Language Arts classes in consecutive (back-to-back) periods. Classes generally meet for two days out of the four-day rotational schedule, with one class rotating out of the block. Every effort is made to provide the two teachers with a common prep period.

RIDGEWOOD HIGH SCHOOL INTERDISCIPLINARY COURSES FOR U.S. HISTORY

- U.S. History 1 and 2: American Humanities
- U.S. History 1 and 2: The American Experience
- U.S. History 1 and 2: American History & American Literature
- U.S. History 1 and 2: American Studies
- History of American Society & Culture

American Humanities: Although many states require three years of social studies in grades 9–12, New Jersey students have the unique opportunity of studying U.S. History for two consecutive years. The American Humanities course is a two-year course with college-prep students enrolled in English and history courses with a thematic curriculum. It is a project-based learning experience using the critical content of American history and literature from the colonial period to the end of the nineteenth century. These themes investigate the American experience through multiple perspectives, understanding the complexities of historical continuity and change through the contemporary connections of settlement, conflict, human rights, revolutionary changes, and competitive ideas. The interdisciplinary connections allow students to use digital photography, coding, robotics, music, and art and science in their study of history and English literature. This model provides a comprehensive learning experience for students and their understanding of the foundational principles of American democracy, immigration and population patterns, building the infrastructure of our country, and conflict. The perspective of literature, art, and music provides a tapestry for understanding the American identity and the struggle for equality.

The American Experience: This flagship course is also a two-year required course with designated teachers for English and social studies in back-to-back periods. Students must demonstrate intellectual curiosity, creative thinking, and their passion for history-related subjects. There is a chronological approach to understanding life in the historical eras of the colonial period, antebellum period, Civil War through Industrialization, world wars and depression, and the contemporary era after 1945. Throughout the year, the two classes meet as one class for guest speakers, presentations, and to explore historical arguments.

American History and American Literature: This honors-level course creatively integrates the fine and performing arts into the study of American history and literature. A team of educators from the English, History, Art and Design, and Performing Arts Departments plan and coordinate the curriculum and program. For example, art teachers visit the English and U.S. History classes to coordinate the study of contemporary arts with each historical period and work of literature. Classes are scheduled back-to-back to allow for extended opportunities for discussion, presentation, and field trip experiences. Students are encouraged to explore creative projects and assignments independently through alternative assessments.

American Studies: This honors-level course is open to students who have demonstrated in grade 9 their ability to handle rigorous and demanding work in research, writing, reading, and presentation. This is an interdisciplinary course with teachers of social studies and English certification. The class meets in back-to-back periods, allowing the teachers to differentiate learning activities and guide students working on long-term projects. The Capstone Seminar model supports a student-driven curriculum, preparing students for the diverse world they are living in. Rubrics for student assessment emphasize inquiry, composition, analysis, and research. The seminar model supports micro-histories and an understanding of the significant threads in American history and society. Students identify areas of research with their teachers and publish position papers supported with primary and secondary sources, literary analysis, and publish a magazine connecting the big picture of American history to current issues. Students who continue for a second year of this course in grade 11 develop evidence-based arguments, research papers, and produce a documentary film.

History of American Society and Culture: This is an interactive learning experience through the study of history, literature, culture, economics, fashion, and music. This is a one-year course beginning with the Progressive Era at the turn of the twentieth century. Students focus on the experiences of women, African Americans, teenagers, immigrants, and laborers and the importance of urbanization in American history. This course is for college-prep students and provides an interdisciplinary experience through guided instruction with their social studies teacher.

INTERDISCIPLINARY INTERNSHIP EXPERIENCE

The Ridgewood Academy for Health Professionals offers an interdisciplinary perspective in collaboration with a local hospital (The Valley Healthcare Network). Students explore issues and perspectives related to public health, science, and literature. In addition to field trips, interactions with professional speakers from the health professionals, and research projects with expert mentors, students have an internship experience. The thematic units throughout the course engage students in inquiry and structured discussions through short stories, poetry, novels, and theatrical plays. The Academy is offered to students in grades 10 and 11, with assignments supporting critical thinking, formal writing, independent research, and an action plan.

The examples of research projects by the students in the Academy for Health Professionals provide evidence of thinking, inquiry, and analysis in a multidisciplinary structure. The interdisciplinary nature of the research projects below provides evidence of science, social issues, behavioral science, and English Language Arts. There is also an interdisciplinary structure connecting high school students with professional mentors. Here are a few examples of capstone seminar research assignments:

- An Interconnected Examination of Health Inequity Cause Factors for Disparities in Cardio-oncology Facing Hispanic and African Communities. Dr. Williams, Horizon Cardiology, mentor.
- High Cost of College Hindering Middle Class Students
- Effects and Feasibility of Stricter Firearm Control for Mentally Ill Individuals in the United States
- The Relationship Between Education and Mental Health Treatment in Ridgewood Adolescents
- Alexis Totaro, Christian Health: Mental Health Services, mentor
- Impacts of Sleep Deprivation as a Result of Excessive Work on Interpersonal Relationships and Psychological Health, Mrs. Suzanne Pearson, Center for Sleep Medicine, mentor
- Effects and Feasibility of Stricter Firearm Control for Mentally Ill Individuals in the United States
- Intermittent fasting and its possible benefits in cancer patients. Nicole Fuller, Nutritionist, Valley Hospital, mentor.
- Providing Effective Care for Babies Born with NAS (Neonatal Abstinence Syndrome)

EXAMPLES OF INTERDISCIPLINARY MODELS FOR SECONDARY SCHOOLS

A. World History Course

An interdisciplinary model for World History should also be considered because of the rich resources in literature, art, music, and architecture. Student learning is enhanced through the reading of literature from different cultural perspectives (African, Indian, Islamic, Japanese, Chinese, Egyptian, Greek, Roman, Byzantine, European, Latin American, Russian) and from the perspectives of different historical eras or periods. There are many connections in world history to literature, music, and civics. The examples below are available on the *Teaching Social Studies* website, sponsored by the New Jersey Council for the Social Studies. https://teachingsocialstudies.org/welcome-page/

The Debate Over Freedom of Religion in World History

Throughout history, people have been persecuted for their religious beliefs. In many cultures, religious institutions are an important part of the culture. However, when individuals or groups express beliefs different from those accepted by the majority and when new populations migrate into a country or culture, they have frequently been persecuted. Although the freedom to worship is considered as a fundamental right by the United Nations Declaration of Human Rights (1948), there continue to be examples of persecution and conflict.

Read the accounts of the persecution and exile experienced by Anne Hutchinson & Roger Williams in colonial America and compare their accounts to the religious zeal expressed in the Taiping Rebellions in China (1850–1867). Have students compare the use of religious images in art (tiger and dragon vs. lamb and dove) between Buddhism and Christianity.

Have a separate group read about the experience of Quakers in West Jersey and Puritans and Presbyterians in East Jersey in the late 17th century. Discover the reasons for the adoption of religious liberty in West Jersey and compare them with the restrictions against atheists in East Jersey.

Engage a third group in reading the accounts of persecution against Christians and others for their beliefs by the Taliban in Afghanistan and the reaction of groups in Afghanistan to the mass killings of Hazara, a Shiite community.

1. To what extent can freedom be restrained?
2. Is it possible to maintain the separation of church and state and legislate morality that is inherent in the religious teachings of specific faiths?
3. Do you think the separation of church and state is essential to a democracy?
4. Apply the lyrics of "Glory" to the meaning of freedom

The Debate Over Equality for Enslaved Persons

The history of the United States was determined by compromises regarding the legislature, property, and the importation of slaves. A controversial compromise was over the counting of enslaved persons in the 13 independent states for purposes of representation and taxation. An agreement was reached to count enslaved persons for the purpose of taxation and representation as only three-fifths of the population. This method of determining representation in the House of Representatives continued until the Thirteenth Amendment abolished slavery.

Slavery was essential to the Brazilian economy. Forty percent of the 10 million enslaved Africans brought to the New World ended up in Brazil. The institution of slavery in Brazil was supported by a majority of white citizens and the Roman Catholic Church. Gradual abolition began in 1871 for children born to enslaved women. Unfortunately, with no plan for assimilation into Brazilian slavery continued into the 20th century with informal agreements for food and housing.

Analyze the Thirteenth Amendment to the Constitution of the United States (1865) and compare it with the Golden Law of 1883 in Brazil.

1. Should the decisions about equality and freedom be determined by governments or by the vote of the citizens?
2. How should decisions be made about the protection of property when property conflicts with human life and personal liberty?
3. Compare the poems of Antonio Goncalves Dias on enslaved people in Brazil. "Cancao do Exilo" (1843), "O navio negreiro" (1880), and "Os escravos" (1883).

B. World History/Global Studies Course

A middle school or high school World History/Global Studies course offers multiple opportunities for interdisciplinary lesson planning with math, science, art, and literature. The *Timetables of History* book provides links to people and events for interdisciplinary lesson planning. (Grun, Bernard, *The Timetables of History,* Simon & Schuster, 1982)

Classical Civilizations

Math: How did the Athenians use geometry to calculate the size of columns and the dimensions of temples?

Science: How were the actors in Greek amphitheaters able to speak to large audiences without assistance?

Art: How does Greek art provide insights and perspectives on Greek culture, society, and history?

Literature: How do excerpts from *The Iliad, The Odyssey, Plato's Republic* and *The Cave,* and *The Clouds* by Aristophanes provide perspectives on the geography, history, and culture of ancient Greece?

Renaissance and Reformation

Math: Calculate the cost of a German guilder to pay for indulgences, the tithe tax to the church, distances between European cities and between Venice and Hormuz or on the Silk Road to China.

Science: Invite a science teacher to discuss the reasons for the controversy of the heliocentric and geocentric universe, how the telescope was made, and miscalculations on the Tower of Pisa.

Art: Invite an art teacher or plan a virtual or in-person trip to a museum to examine Renaissance art, sculpture, fresco paintings, perspective, Byzantine Art, and changes in art over time.

Literature: Read excerpts from Petrarch's sonnets, Boccaccio's *Decameron*, Dante's *Inferno*, Thomas More's *Utopia*, Machiavelli's *The Prince*, and *Praise of Folly* by Erasmus.

C. United States History Course

Development of Transportation in the United States in the Nineteenth Century

Math: Invite a math teacher to discuss the calculations for inclined planes, location of locks on canals, weight canal ships could carry, and distances by land travel and canal.

Science: Invite a science teacher to discuss the design of locks, steam power technology, underground sewer systems, and the functionality of plank and McAdam roads.

Art: Invite an art teacher to discuss and illustrate Hudson River School paintings of canals and canal workers

Literature: Read excerpts from *Fire Worship*, *The Scarlet Letter*, and the *House of Seven Gables* by Nathaniel Hawthorne, *The History and Life of Christopher Columbus* by Washington Irving, and *The Last of the Mohicans* by James Fenimore Cooper.

Civil Rights Era

Music: Listen to the religious hymns, "Onward Christian Soldiers" and "This Little Light of Mine," popular songs "Blowin' in the Wind" by Bob Dylan, and songs that protestors sang in the face of danger, "Going Down to Mississippi" by Phil Ochs.

Art: Introduce your students to the perspective of African American artists on the Civil Rights movement through a virtual tour or presentation by an art teacher or professor. Examples of influential artists are Barbara

Jones-Hugo, Marie Johnson-Calloway, Alvin D. Loving, Jr., and Barkley L. Hendricks.

Literature: Introduce your students to the writing of excerpts from James Baldwin's *Sonny's Blues*, to understand the perspective of addiction and incarceration, and the themes of music and family in the Black community and Maya Angelou's *Caged Bird*.

Science: Invite a psychology teacher or professor to explain the "Doll Study" by Kenneth and Mamie Clark that influenced the *Brown v. Board of Education* Supreme Court decision and the contributions of Katherine Johnson to the NASA space program

INDEPENDENT STUDY, COLLEGE PARTNERSHIPS

Some high school history or social studies departments are limited in the size of their student population, the experience of the faculty may be limited, and flexible scheduling is not a viable option. These are real challenges, but they should not justify the failure to implement a comprehensive interdisciplinary educational experience for students in your high school.

Consider an independent study option for students with a demonstrated ability for inquiry, research, and a commitment to work. An independent study option can be for a quarter or marking period, over a one-week vacation period, or over the summer. When providing independent study outside of the school day, consider offering one credit or recognition on the student's transcript.

The independent study should have a faculty mentor and be evaluated by a public or professional panel. Consider an educator from another school or district, a college professor, a recent graduate, or a local historian.

Examples of independent study projects that are interdisciplinary are:

Fashion	NASA Space Program
Harlem Renaissance	Hudson River School
American Television	Broadway Musicals
Photography	Historical Legacy of Your Local Community
American Automobile	Lifestyle of Teenagers in Specific Decades

Another option for high schools with limited resources is to partner with professors at local colleges. Most colleges have an American Studies department and are a valuable resource for curriculum and guest speakers.

WHAT CAN WE DO?

Teacher educators may be reluctant to take on the revisions to their courses (and shifts in philosophy) that would be required for a truly interdisciplinary approach to preservice education. And truthfully, there are many existing barriers to such an approach, outlined above. An essential change that has to be made in preservice teacher education programs involves planning lessons and units with preservice and experienced teachers in other disciplines. For example, when planning an interdisciplinary lesson or unit on the solutions to climate change or environmental pollution, social studies preservice teachers should collaborate with math and science teachers. When planning an interdisciplinary lesson or unit on child labor legislation in the Progressive Era, social studies preservice teachers should collaborate with English and literature teachers.

Conceivably, then, it may fall to preservice educators themselves to follow through on this goal. Students should take as many opportunities as they can to broaden their own educational experiences, beyond the classroom (e.g., study abroad experiences), and to take full advantage of the various field placements already featured in their programs by visiting other teachers from other disciplines. Seeing how subject areas beyond one's own experiences in the classroom, and how frequently those subjects may connect to other topics, is vital to develop both a sense of and commitment to interdisciplinary education.

This sort of "grassroots" approach is contrary to the manner in which most educational reform over the past few decades has been designed and implemented, typically in the form of "top-down" mandates or policies. But if interdisciplinary pedagogy is more than a set of topics and skills, and is instead a frame of mind that teachers adopt and nurture, then "from the bottom up" has the most potential for success. Preservice educators don't have to wait for their colleges and departments to catch up; they can take the initiative on their own.

REFERENCES

Applebee, A., Burroughs, R., and Cruz, G. (2000). Curricular conversations in elementary school classrooms: Case studies of interdisciplinary instruction. In S. Wineburg and P. Grossman (Eds.), *Interdisciplinary curriculum: Challenges to implementation*. Teachers College Press: New York, 93–111.

Austin, A. (2003). Historic battles. *The Christian Science Monitor,* October 21, 2003. Retrieved from http://www.csmonitor.com/2003/1021/p13s02-legn.html

Hansen, M., Levesque, E., Valant, J., and Quintero, D. (2018). *The 2018 Brown Center report on American education: How well are American students learning?*

The Brookings Institute. Retrieved from https://www.brookings.edu/wp-content/uploads/2018/06/2018-Brown-Center-Report-on-American-Education_FINAL1.pdf

Klein, J.T. (2006). A platform for a shared discourse of interdisciplinary education. *Journal of Social Science Education, 5* (4), 10–18.

Lee, J.K. (2005). Reconsidering the debate: Social studies, history, and academic disciplines. *International Journal of Social Education, 20* (1), 61–62.

Oberdörfer, S., Birnstiel, S., Latoschik, M.E., and Grafe, S. (2021). Mutual benefits: Interdisciplinary education of pre-service teachers and HCI students in VR/AR learning environment design. *Frontiers in Education.* Retrieved from https://www.frontiersin.org/articles/10.3389/feduc.2021.693012/full

Risinger, C.F. (2005). Social studies, interdisciplinary teaching, and technology. *Social Education, 69* (4), 149–150.

Safire, W. (1993, March 7). On language: Dog's breakfast. *The New York Times,* March 7, 1993, section 6, p. 16. Retrieved from https://www.nytimes.com/1993/03/07/magazine/on-language-dog-s-breakfast.html

Stodolsky, S.S., Salk, S., and Glaessner, B. (1991). Student views about learning math and social studies. *American Educational Research Journal, 28* (1), 89–116.

Thacker, E.S., and Bodle, A.T. (2022). Seizing the moment: A critical place-based partnership for antiracist elementary social studies teacher education. *Theory & Research in Social Education.* https://doi.org/10.1080/00933104.2022.2075296

Wiggins, G. (2015). Fixing high school by listening to students. Retrieved from http://www.teachthought.com/learning/fixing-high-school-listening-to-students/

Wineburg, S. (1997). Beyond breadth and depth: Subject matter knowledge and assessment. *Theory Into Practice, 36* (4), 255–261.

Chapter 6

Conclusion

Sandra Zak

The goal of this text was not to replace the many other books on teaching interdisciplinary methods. The few that we have are meant to be used in a school of education setting that seeks to teach preservice teachers the method. Rather, this text seeks to provide a source that will appeal to the many different groups making up our system of education. This includes the following but is certainly not a complete list: university faculty, preservice and in-service teachers, administrators, professional development facilitators, and many others who are involved in education. In this spirit, chapters of the text were written by university faculty delivering courses, along with teachers in both elementary and high school who have successfully used the teaching method in innovative ways and without any training.

Chapter 2 begins with a description of the Interdisciplinary Studies in Elementary Education major at Monmouth University. The focus of the major is on teaching students broad and deep content knowledge in all the academic areas needed in their future classrooms. This expertise gives these students a major advantage compared with single-major students. They have the potential to comfortably teach all the major academic areas in the elementary classroom. They also have the ability to teach, with a passing Praxis score, in the appropriate middle school subject. Additionally, they have the chance to bring this knowledge together into the capstone course. As we have noted, while the program certainly deserves interest, it will not equally apply to every person reading this book. A university faculty member or administrator may see this as a model program and bring it, or some modified version to their school. An elementary school administrator may look at the course offerings and may change their hiring practices, looking for preservice teachers with added breadth and deep content knowledge. However, it is the final course, addressed in detail in the last portion of this chapter, which will serve all the different groups reading this text. The details of the chapter walks the reader through the selection of a topic, with outside speakers providing the ideas. The requirement is to learn more about the topic, through a literature review. The students are then encouraged to build a web design for their unit topic, where they can see how each of the academic subjects are connected and the learning standards are displayed. Actual student work is shown, providing examples of what a fully complete web design looks like. It is this capstone course, its descriptions of how it runs and the work it produces that will engage all the different readers of this text. A university or a professional developer will find a way to teach interdisciplinary methods or bring them to current teachers. School administrators will have a better understanding of what an interdisciplinary lesson is, how it is built, structured, and most importantly, how it teaches the required standards.

Chapter 3 provides us with another way to look at designing and implementing an interdisciplinary unit. Here, the idea of web design is replaced with graphic organizers. Then, the backward design approach is applied to create the unit plan. We then see different examples of planned, developed, and taught interdisciplinary unit plans. The example of the lighthouse provided rich geography and engineering work by the students, and the problem-solving competition, Odyssey of the Mind, allowed the students to access and use their most creative talents. Both show the possibility of learning in depth, the connections to the learning standards, and the fun the students have engaging in these projects. This chapter will apply to all our parties, but in-service teachers will find so much to take with them. Seeing a fellow educator work out a systematic way to teach an engaging unit plan that involves the many different standards will show teachers in the field that first-hand knowledge that only a fellow peer can share.

Chapter 4 begins with a detailed look at a Standards Model used in an interdisciplinary unit on the responsibilities of K–2 students as global citizens. The detail the author provides in the standards covered gives us an idea of just how broad and deep this teaching method is. The standards span Civics, Economics, Climate, and ELA. We see ideas on how global warming affects our economy. It provides ways for students to become involved by participating in problem-solving and decision-making activities. The second example given is an Assessment Model for grades 3–5 on the geography of New Jersey. With the topic, it appears the author will only be working in social studies, but then the author shows the natural connections to ELA, science, and even art as the unit progresses. Finally, a third unit is discussed for grades 3–5, on Economic Financial literacy. Here we see again the breadth of material that needs to be covered to understand the topic, from ELA, Economics, and Mathematics. The author makes clear that so many topics, when thought about naturally, are interdisciplinary and, when taught this way, provide better learning for the students and more retention of knowledge. While this chapter provides a rich set of examples for all our readers, a school administration will find this of particular interest in its demonstration of deep learning and the standards being covered.

In the last chapter of the text, the interdisciplinary method is discussed at the secondary level. In no way is this chapter a complete guide for readers. It is only a beginning to the question: how do we implement this method of teaching into a system where each academic subject exists within itself? In the first part, we see how an undergraduate school of education is bringing together all their preservice secondary majors to look at common issues they will all face. This is the first step in the process of letting students in vastly different majors reflect on how their futures will look similar rather than just at the differences. This first step may appear small in consideration of the full-blown program discussed in chapter 2. However, we must recognize the giant step is to bring together secondary math, science, English, and social studies majors into one class and get them to see how they are all more similar to each other than not. A step of this sort opens the door to further projects and ideas. For instance, the students could be paired with a different major and asked to write about a topic that they find common ground on. From this, it would be a natural next step to ask students in the pairing to write a lesson plan to teach the common topic. While this would be a more multidisciplinary approach, it would still fall under the umbrella of interdisciplinary teaching. This is just one way to get the students at the secondary level to start seeing the natural connections between their subjects. Many more ideas are possible, but the first step of getting the students in the same class is required. These authors point to a powerful way to accomplish this. As the chapter continues, we again see an in-service teacher determined to bring a new and better way of learning into the classroom. The teacher wishes to reach his students through the use of a trending topic, the movie *Titanic*. While not a major historical event, it nonetheless provided fertile ground for bringing in many different disciplines. These included social class, immigration, and ethical issues, along with some science and even mathematics. All of this was accomplished by a single educator using popular culture to teach popular culture and use it to teach a vast array of disciplines. This social studies teacher, whose discipline spans many different subjects, realized the power of putting these together. The next step would be for those down the hall in English to align with this by assigning a reading that would would integrate this material. The science wing could study not just the freezing of seawater but the formation of large icebergs and their movements. Finally, the study of the mathematical aspects of the design of ships. In the last portion of this chapter, we have Ridgewood High School giving an example of an entire department of social studies teachers coming together so they can create an interdisciplinary set of courses. Once again, we see social studies teachers leading the way, using their unique knowledge of many disciplines. Going forward, other schools may read this, and maybe mathematics and science departments will reconsider their courses and how they can be taught in a more interdisciplinary way. The same with the other subjects combining to create courses that connect and touch on multiple topics while infusing naturally the ideas of multiple disciplines. The discussion has begun, and what is possible is still in the future. All the readers at the secondary level should see the value of these beginning ideas and use them to create future learning environments that engage our students in interdisciplinary units that represent real-world learning.

About the Editors and Authors

Jiwon Kim is an associate professor of educational foundations and social studies education at Monmouth University, where she has taught courses in foundations, social studies methods, and interdisciplinary instruction for social and global sustainable issues. She received her PhD degree from Purdue University. As a founding director, she was involved in designing and coordinating the Interdisciplinary Studies for Elementary Educators program. She also served as a faculty representative to the United Nations. Prior to her work in teacher education, she was a researcher at national educational institutes in South Korea, where she participated in developing educational policy and national curriculum. Her publications include articles in *Teacher Educator*, *Journal of Moral Education*, and *Education and Culture*. She has served on multiple editorial boards, including *Teaching Social Studies*, a joint publication of the New York and New Jersey State Councils for Social Studies Education. Her practice and study of interdisciplinary education have been presented through many college courses and state and international workshops for educators.

Sandra Zak teaches mathematics, mathematics education, and interdisciplinary studies at Monmouth University. Her research is focused on using social justice and culturally relevant teaching practices for preservice teachers majoring in mathematics and interdisciplinary studies in elementary education. She has written curricula for interdisciplinary projects with fellow university colleagues and has work in preparation to be published on Latinx stereotypes, diversity, and food waste. She has spoken at conferences including the Association of Mathematics Teachers of New Jersey, the Mathematical Association of America, and the Comparative and International Education Society, and she has been the recipient of many grants, including a New Jersey State IMPACT Grant.

About the Editors and Authors

CONTRIBUTING AUTHORS

Hank Bitten is currently the executive director of the New Jersey Council for the Social Studies (www.njcss.org) located at Rutgers University. He taught social studies at Martin Luther High School in Maspeth, Ridgewood High School, and served as a district supervisor at Ramapo Indian Hills High School in Bergen County. He was an adjunct professor at Concordia College, Bronxville, New York; Fairleigh Dickinson University; Montclair University; and Ramapo College of New Jersey. He was the founder and director of the Lutheran School of Flushing (1974–1980), the New Jersey Council for History Education, director for two Teaching American History Grants with the U.S. Department of Education, consultant with the U.S. Department of Education on History Education programs, and the director of two grants on curriculum for the 250th anniversary of the American Revolution. Through his leadership with the NJ Council for Social Studies, New Jersey adopted a K–12 climate education curriculum and a requirement to teach civics in middle school. He lives in Oakland, New Jersey, with his wife Elaine, has two married children, and five grandchildren. He is a graduate of Concordia University and New York University.

Christine Grabowski has been an elementary school teacher in the Hazlet Township School District in New Jersey since 1996. She serves as the administrative aide, teacher leader, and novice teacher mentor in the Hazlet Schools. Christine is also an adjunct professor, clinical faculty supervisor, and professional development school liaison at Monmouth University. She earned a bachelor's degree in Elementary Education and Psychology from Rowan University, a master's degree in Teaching from Marygrove College, and is a graduate of the NJ Excel Program, earning a Supervisor and Principal Certificate.

Mark Pearcy is a professor of social studies education at Rider University in Lawrenceville, New Jersey. He teaches undergraduate methods courses and is a student teacher supervisor. Prior to this, he taught high school social studies classes for nineteen years and earned National Board Certification. His research interests include American history education, civic literacy, racial residential segregation, and the "just war" doctrine. Email: mpearcy@rider.edu

Vecihi Serbay Zambak, PhD, is an associate professor of mathematics education in the Department of Curriculum and Instruction. Zambak directs the mathematics programs and serves as the program director of Interdisciplinary Studies for Educators. Prior to joining Monmouth, he taught secondary mathematics in private and public high schools in Istanbul, Turkey, and in the Netherlands. He earned his Master of Science degree in Mathematics and Science Education from the University of Amsterdam, where his thesis focused on a quasi-experimental study of ninth-grade students' mathematical reasoning with numerical systems. Both his doctoral and post-doctoral studies at Clemson University and Marquette University focused on preparation and development for STEM teachers. His research interests center around STEM teachers' professional noticing, argumentation skills, content learning with technology, and interdisciplinary teaching practices.

www.ingramcontent.com/pod-product-compliance
Lightning Source LLC
Chambersburg PA
CBHW021813220426
43662CB00006B/298